LIVING EVERYDAY INSPIRED WITH QUOTES AND WISDOM FROM GREAT THINKERS, BOOKS, ETC.

RUDOLPH MENSAH

365 DAYS OF INSPIRATION: LIVING EVERYDAY INSPIRED WITH QUOTES AND WISDOM FROM GREAT THINKERS, BOOKS, ETC.

BY

RUDOLPH MENSAH

+233 247 930 389

rudolphmensah87@gmail.com

rudolph@rudolphmensah.com

Website: http://www.rudolphmensah.com/

Blog:

http://www.rudolphmensah.com/blog

Kindly join my mailing list:
http://eepurl.com/c0KDCf

Discover other titles by **Rudolph Mensah** at his **Amazon author** page:

http://www.amazon.com/author/rudolphmensah

COPYRIGHT © 2018, RUDOLPH MENSAH

I have tried my best to credit the original owners of the quotes, any oversight or misquote is wholly accepted by me. I would be glad to hear from you on any of the quote I credited to the wrong person and I would gladly make the changes.

Again, no book recommendation I made was paid endorsement, I simply benefited from the books and decided to share them with you.

Reviewers may quote brief passages in reviews.

DEDICATION

This one is for every man or woman who has ever lived and left us with their wisdom. For the people who are alive today and are leaving us wisdom in their messages, the world is better because of you.

To George Weir, you might have to tell me to stop dedicating everything I write to you but then I won't stop because you are at the centre of it all. I don't have a story without the story of a man who has dedicated his life to making others life meaningful. This one is also for you.

To all my teachers, from kindergarten to University, I am here because of you. If you are reading this, thank you.

CONTENTS

365 Days of Inspiration

I have loved reading and collecting inspirational and motivational quotes from people all over the world. There are times I read quotes from those who have influenced our world and it sum up what they stood for. These are the wisdom and knowledge passed down from great men and women from time immemorial to our generation. These quotes help us to find our path and stay on it. As a personal development author and inspirational speaker, I have used these quotes in my books and speeches because they carry timeless wisdom. I therefore strongly believe that we can learn from these quotes not only wisdom but the mistakes as well as the things which made these great people successful.

I have therefore carefully collected 365 of the most profound and thought provoking motivational and inspirational quotes I have encountered, one for each day of the year. Before you step out, there is a quote for the day, to motivate you and help you stay on track to becoming your dream.

Some of them are by great people you may know, others by people you probably haven't heard of and I have added a few of my own quotes I believe will spice up each day of your life.

I know they will be of great resource to you and help put you in a good mood for your day.

Thank you for buying this book and may each day of the year bring you happiness and fulfillment.

Rudolph Mensah

Speaker, Author & Doctor (MH)

JANUARY

It's the first month of the year. Perhaps, last year didn't end well, but this is a fresh start. Let's make the best out of the month. As always, set your goals and hunt them. Have the best of the year by starting strong.

DAY 1

"Today is the first day of the rest of your life."

We begin this year with lots of enthusiasm, hopes and dreams. I spent time following peoples' resolutions for the year as they shared them online.

I shared with my followers and friends about the need to develop more discipline for their year instead of setting up resolutions. What we need more is to be disciplined in our daily life.

You may not be reading this book on the first day of the year. You may be reading this book on a cold day, hot day or a rainy day; whatever the weather, whatever situation you find yourself in; whether you are struggling with failure or enjoying success, begin with the belief, that today, whichever day it is, is the first day of the rest of your life.

This stark realization and acceptance of today as the first day of the rest of our life will bring us to the point of accepting our state and subsequently taking responsibility of the direction, our lives will go from here. What happened a year ago isn't a problem, your past isn't an issue, what matters is the decision to change the direction of your life.

So, don't look back, you are not going that way. Now, choose a new path, decide to become a new person and resolve to focus on the future you imagine. Let's make the rest of our lives the best of our lives.

DAY 2

"Step out of the history that is holding you back. Step into the new story you are willing to create."

Oprah Winfrey; Media Proprietor & Talk Show Host.

As we make the decision to go in the direction of our dreams and forge a new future for ourselves, the first thing we have to do is to leave the past.

Be willing to let not the past define you but refine you. I have always reckoned that our history shouldn't define our future. We all have histories, we all have a chapter in our story we wouldn't want to read out loud.

We have a scene in our lives we wouldn't want to see play on the screens, we will bow down our heads in shame if it does but what happened in the past wasn't to hold us at ransom and stop us from going into our future.

Don't let your history interfere with your future. Own it, learn from it, let it refine you, now, go out today with the renewed hope and belief in the coming future.

DAY 3

"A journey of a thousand miles begin with a single step."

Lao Tzu; Philosopher.

I had often looked at an enormous task ahead and given up in my mind because I imagined how hard it was going to be. I changed my mindset over a few years ago and began to rather do something small every day in the direction of my dream and that has changed my life significantly.

We often look at how far we have to go and give up instead of taking inspiration from how far we have come. We have been made aware of making the decision to own our history and taking the responsibility of going in a new direction this year.

It's a process and requires persistent action. Don't worry about how long you have to do it, just begin. Picasso once said, "action is the foundation for success". You can plan, postulate, strategize but if you don't take action by taking the first step then you will never move forward in life.

I never knew I will be writing books, speaking to various audiences, but I took the first step and I am on a path to my dreams. This book began with just one quote till I get to quote number 365.

So, today, go out there and take the first step into your dreams.

DAY 4

"Twenty years from now you will be more disappointed by the things you didn't do than the ones you did do. So, throw off the bowlines. Sail away from the safe harbour. Catch the trade winds in your sails. Explore. Dream. Discover".

Mark Twain; Writer, Humourist, Lecturer.

For most people, they never get to live their lives because they wait too long to even begin it. An unknown writer once wrote the words,

"Oh God! only to reach the point of death and realize that we have been living our lives wrong." How tragic?

What are you afraid of?
That you will make mistakes?
Mistakes are proof that you are trying something.

That you will fail?
It means you tried, most people won't even dare.
So, go out there today and make every minute count.

Do something that you will thank yourself for in the future. Don't look back 20 years and regret not doing something you should have done.
Grow up with memories not regrets. Let's go out today with the determination to begin the life we dream of.

DAY 5

"Faith is taking the first step even when you don't see the whole staircase."

Martin Luther King Jr.; Civil Right Activist.

There is a Chinese proverb which says: "The person who deliberates fully before taking a step will spend his entire life on one leg."

You can't figure it all out at once. Just start. Sometimes, we like to over analyze situations and end up in a spiral of doing nothing. Too much analysis leads to paralysis. You have to take a leap and grow your wings down.

We have been told a journey of a thousand miles begin with a single step, we can only take that first step in faith. We may not know where that step will take us but with faith we can begin a new journey which will lead us to our glorious future. What is it you want to achieve this year and beyond? Go online, go to YouTube, learn something about it, read about it, go to seminars, just do something about it. This is not time to over-think and keep analyzing, take that step and see how you progress.

One of my goals this year is to write a movie script, I have spent the first few weeks of the year learning from tutorials on YouTube on how to write a script. Just take the first step, something small today and then something small tomorrow will be getting you closer to what you seek.

DAY 6

---

*"It's not the absence of fear, it's overcoming it.
Sometimes you've got to blast through and have faith."*

Emma Watson; Actress, Model and Activist.

Someone once said, "feel the fear and do it anyway". Wasn't I afraid when I published my first book? Wasn't I afraid it would come out and people will reject me and my work?

Did I not have any sense of fear when I published the second, third and fourth books on Amazon? I did. Pressing the "publish" button on Amazon was scary. I know, this is not to be compared to the fears we face in our lives. Trust me, growing up in a village in Ghana, I can tell you the countless number of times I have encountered various degrees of fear.

Of course, we all face fear and fear is a necessary factor in life. The point is, should it stop us from pursuing our dreams? The only way to overcome the fear is to go out there with faith as we learned yesterday.

As you go out today, don't let fear hold you by the neck and strangle you to death. Fear of failure, fear of ridicule, fear of embarrassment, listen, we are all bound to suffer a level of defeat and embarrassment in life but those who succeed are those who don't allow these things to define them.

As we begin this new journey, we should always remind ourselves, we will feel the fear but it shouldn't stop us.

Let's blast through the fear with faith.

DAY 7

"The most difficult thing is the decision to act, the rest is merely tenacity."

Amelia Earhart; American Aviation Pioneer and Author.

There is always hesitancy in starting. Jimmy Wales, Co-founder of Wikipedia once said; **"Just start, don't be a talker. Don't worry about if you are perfect or not. The sooner you get started, the sooner you'll get somewhere."**

We often stare so much at the task ahead we are crippled by fear and indecision.

Whatever your dream is, whatever your goal is, make the decision today to act. Just start, don't worry about being perfect from the start. The sooner you begin, the sooner you will learn and grow your knowledge.

Indecision is very fatiguing and can delay our progress in life. Imagine walking in the middle of the road, you will get knocked down by a car. You have to decide which side of the road you will walk. The left or the right side. You may not have all the fact to decide which side to take but either side of the road is less dangerous than walking in the middle.

So is life, you have to decide to act and stop running away from making a decision which is a decision most people make.

What is it you want to achieve this year? Decide to act, now, today.

DAY 8

"Champions aren't made in the gyms. Champions are made from something they have deep inside them-desire, dream, a vision."

Muhammad Ali; Professional Boxer and Activist.

People are rewarded in public for what they do in private. We see a winner on stage receiving an award and we think that's all there is to winning. The public glory is all we see, the media shows us mountain climbers when they are on top of the mountain, smiling and excited.

They never show us when they fell down on the way up, when someone slipped and almost died, the struggle on the way to the top is hidden from the public so we are oblivious to the process of winning.

It is a process and the daily relentless pursuit of our dreams bring us glory. Practice, keep practicing and keep getting better. Deliberate consistent practice makes you a champion. When others are having a good time, you put on your shirt and go for training. When others are sleeping, I open my laptop and start writing, it doesn't matter how many words I write, I just write. Soon, I turn out a book and put it out there, what do people see? My name on a book and they think that's all there is, no, there have been hours and hours of hard work behind the scenes.

It is the desire to succeed, to make other people's lives better and the vision to keep working everyday towards my purpose which drives me.

It doesn't happen in a classroom, it doesn't happen in a gym, it happens because you have something deep inside you, what dream, what desire, what vision drives you?

DAY 9

"I can accept failure. Everyone fails at something but I can't accept not trying."

Michael Jordan; Retired Professional Basketball Player & Businessman.

We all fail in life but the question is, who gets back up? I am determined to win but I am also prepared to lose. I don't fear failing, I fear not trying.

Fear, someone said, "is the most destructive of all human diseases".

Fear cripples a lot of people to never come out and do what they feel in their hearts they are supposed to do.

Most people don't have the gut to fail and if you afraid to lose, you have no right to win.

It's hard to fail but it's worst to regret not trying. You will always wonder what could have happened if I tried?

The pain of regret is worse than the pain of failing. You can always learn your lessons and try again when you fail.

Don't allow fear to stop you in your tracks. Walk out today with confidence in yourself and abilities. Hold your head up.

DAY 10

The battles that count aren't the ones for gold medals. The struggles within yourself-the invisible, inevitable battles inside all of us-that's where it's at."

G. Jesse Owens; Athlete.

Self-discipline is a major determinant of success. Our mind is a battlefield and those who make the best of life are those who are able to conquer themselves, master their emotions and their minds.

We have to decide whether to wake up early or not, to train or not, to practice or not, these are examples of daily decisions we need to make in order to win.

If a man can master his own body, develop self-discipline and positive work ethics then success is a must.

Slay your demons, the things that easily entangle you and make it difficult for you to succeed. This is how you reposition yourself to succeed. In order to win, you need to win the battles inside of you. You have to win in your mind before you can win in life.

DAY 11

"It isn't where you came from, it's where
you're going that counts."

Ella Fitzgerald, Singer.

I have always believed in my future. I grew up in a village in Ghana I still call home and I have never been doubtful of the fact that from this small village I am going all over the world to make impact.

I believe it is the belief in where you are going which is even much more important than where you are coming from. Many people use their geographical location as an excuse to fail in life. Your location isn't an issue, it is true that where you are right now may deny you of certain opportunities but none of that count and all that matters is your decision to move yourself in the direction you want.

It may be harder, it may take longer, you may have to fight more battles but if you believe in yourself and where you envision yourself to be, you will get there.

Let's keep walking. Don't stop now, we shall win, maybe not immediately but definitely.

DAY 12

"The beautiful thing about learning is that no one can take it away from you".

G B. B King; Musician.

My father always told me that. He often used that as the reason why he isn't leaving us any lands or properties. He would say, "his family members would take the land from us after his death." That of course was his excuse.

Everything I learned myself, I remember and no one can take it away from me. Self-education is therefore the most important thing anyone can do for himself or herself in my opinion. This drives my insatiable desire to read every day.

I love reading because the more I read the more I come to understand myself and the world I live in which is a requirement for success.

So, today, read, learn and get into your mind something that no one can take away from you.

DAY 13

"Optimism is the faith that leads to achievement."

Helen Adams Keller; Author, Political activist & Lecturer.

I believe no one knows enough to be a pessimist. There are things in life which were deemed impossible only because of limited knowledge and ignorance.

Remaining highly optimistic in a negative environment is an ingredient for success. We must remain positive and optimistic about the future.

It is difficult to remain optimistic especially when the physical environment suggests otherwise, when things are not going as planned, many will be forced to give up but the highly optimistic beings always hold on to their convictions even in the midst of failure and that is how they succeed.

Remain optimistic today about your dreams. Let's hold on to the faith that things will change and will change for the better. This will keep us working on our dreams with faith and belief. Don't be in despair, keep the faith till we make it. We shall win, maybe not immediately but definitely.

DAY 14

"Hold fast to dreams, for if dreams die, life is
a broken winged bird that cannot fly."

Langston Hughes; Poet.

I believe in my dreams, I will make every one of my dreams
possible and that is why I live. The day I lose the believe in my
dreams, what is there to live for?

I dream of giving my mum everything life can offer, I dream
of impacting my generation, I dream of making healthcare
affordable, accessible and available for all Africans, I dream
about changing my world from negativity and hatred to
positivity and love. I keep going every day because of these
dreams, the day I lose these dreams, what else am I living for?

So, today, whatever dreams you have, whatever your dream, it
may seem like a long shot, it may even seem like you will never
get there but hold on to it. Keep the faith and believe that
your dreams will one day come true if you don't stop chasing
them. Keep running after your dreams. There is no
prosthetic for an amputated dream, keep the blood
supply to your dream alive.

DAY 15

"I challenge you to make your life masterpiece. I challenge you to join the ranks of those people who live what they teach, who walk their talk.

Anthony Robbins; Author, entrepreneur, philanthropist and life coach.

One great American, Thomas Paine, in his book COMMON SENSE, had a powerful line:

"I choose not to be a common man."

This is a bold assertion. Becoming great, becoming what you dream of is a choice and once you make that choice to become great, you set yourself apart from the masses. You have to first decide you don't like where you are now and you have the responsibility to get yourself to where you dream of. When you make this decision, your whole being begins to align with this new mindset.

It's a decision. It's a choice you have to make. So, let today be the day you decide to make your life a masterpiece. Don't settle for mediocrity.

You are made for more, don't settle for less.

DAY 16

"Make the most of yourself by fanning the
tiny, inner sparks of possibility into flames of
achievement."

Golda Meir; Israeli teacher, stateswoman &
the fourth Prime Minister of Israel.

Success doesn't happen overnight. It happens overtime. It
requires working consistently on yourself to become the
person you were meant to be.

It is our responsibility to keep fanning into flames these sparks
of possibility, the belief that we can do it. The belief that if
others have done it then we can also do it.

If people from your country, race, community, if other human
beings have done it then it is a testament that you can also
accomplish what you set yourself to achieve.

Whatever we do today should be keeping this hope alive,
holding on to our faith that our dreams are possible.

No one will fan them for you, it is your job to keep this belief
alive every day. Even when things seem contrary to what we
belief, keep fanning.

If others have done it, then we can also do it. It is this belief
which keeps our head above water till we get ashore.

DAY 17

"Your goals are the road maps that guide you
and show you what is possible for your life."

Les Brown; Author & Motivational Speaker.

I have goals and my goals are landmarks on the road to my dreams. Every day, when I accomplish a goal, I am persuaded I am on the right way to my dreams. I develop a new sense of confidence and belief that I can accomplish more. Without goals, you may lose sight of where you are going and you will also lose your self-belief. The accomplishment of each goal is an indication and a signal that everything else before me is also possible.

When I accomplished my goal of writing my first book, I became fully persuaded and confident of writing more books and then becoming a speaker when I started talking about my book and sharing the inspiration with others.

I again began a new path of writing new books, this is book number 5 in a year. With each new goal I set for myself, it moves me closer to the ultimate dream. With every goal accomplished, it ignites the possibility of becoming more. We need goals to keep us on the road.
What is your goal for today, this week, this month and this year?

DAY 18

"No dreamer is ever too small; no dream is
ever too big."

Unknown

Before I published my book BECOMING YOUR DREAM, I had a lot of people telling me I am too young to write a book telling other people how to become what they dreamed of when they didn't even know my target audience and what the book was about.

People told me to wait on it. To write the book in five or ten years. They told me it was too big a title for a book to be coming from such a young person.

Others felt I shouldn't publish a book. A lot more said it was a risk. I should just concentrate starting out in life not to take up the risk of publishing a book which will become unsuccessful.

I had my dream and I believed in my dream. I went ahead anyway with support from my mentor and trusted friends and family members. Don't let others try to talk you out of the dream you have because they feel it's too big. If they say your dreams are too big, sometimes that's because they think too small.

DAY 19

"Beware of monotony; it's the mother of all
the deadly sins."

Edith Wharton; Novelist.

John C. Maxwell said in his book **TODAY MATTERS,**
"Your life will only change when you change something you
do every day. The day I read that, I spend hours meditating
and thinking about how true that is. Later, I learned that about
90% of what we do every day we do out of habit, which also
means we do them without thinking.

Until we become conscious of what we do daily and make a
deliberate effort to change it, we will likely end up the same.

Change will happen when we take the responsibility to change
our daily routine. We wake up, same time, do the same things
over and over again expecting something different, something
Albert Einstein describes as insanity.

Challenge yourself today to challenge your routine. Do
something different, read a book, write a to do list and change
how you go about your day.
Let us challenge our routine today. Pay attention to what you
do daily and then bring yourself to break the monotony.

DAY 20

"You got a dream, you gotta protect it. People can't do something themselves, they wanna tell you you can't do it. If you want something, go get it. Period."

Will Smith; Pursuit of Happiness (Movie).

This is a movie which has changed lives, inspired a lot of people and here is one of my favorite lines in the movie by Will Smith. People quickly impose their limitations on you. Don't accept them. The fact that someone failed doesn't mean you will also fail.

Kofi Annan, a former UN Secretary-General once said, "…never doubt your capacity to triumph where others have not."

Worst of it, some people never tried it themselves but someone told them it is not possible so they also tell everyone it is not possible.

Protect your dream from mediocre minds. Don't be limited by other people's limitations.

DAY 21

"History shows us that the people who end up changing the world – the great political, social, scientific, technological, artistic, even sports revolutionaries – are always nuts, until they are right, and then they are geniuses."

John Eliot; Novelist & Screenwriter.

Don't worry if people call you crazy for what you are doing, you are in a good company. Not everyone will see what you see so don't worry if they think you are going nut. My friends and family thought I was wasting my time and money on books, reading books all the time, going for seminars, conferences. Why not just concentrate on my profession, work, get money, marry and have some kids?

That is the normal life and I am not normal. If you want to live the life society has carved out for you, then go ahead but if you want to be different then they will call you crazy, deal with it. Don't worry about it. In the end, they will all applaud you.

Don't be limited by what others say, you will never be defeated by what others say as long as you belief in yourself and what you are doing, keep working. You shall be rewarded.

DAY 22

"If you don't risk anything, you risk even more."

Erica Jong; Novelist.

Life itself is a risk. To live we risk dying. No one is getting out of here alive. When we want to live a risk-free life, we are basically saying we want to remain just as we are.

Many are held back by the fear of losing and never venture into anything with the slightest risk. Afraid of making mistakes, afraid of being embarrassed, afraid of losing, afraid of not reaching the goal.

Don't let the risk stop you. It doesn't mean just go out there and take risk, take intelligent and calculated risks. Learn how to take risk. This subject has been highly discussed by many self-development experts.

If you don't jump, you won't fall but what is the use of your life if you spend all your time on the ground? Then why did you even come here?

Remember, we are going to achieve great things this year. In order to do that, we need to take risk.

DAY 23

"If you don't like the road you're walking, start paving another one."

Dolly Parton, Singer & Songwriter.

Life is all about choices, at every point in time, we have the choice of taking the responsibility to change the course of our lives or remaining on the same path. it doesn't happen overnight but we can take a new step in the direction we want to go if we want to change.

Complaining and whining will never help you. If you don't like the life you are living, if you are not happy with your current situation, you have the power and responsibility to make a change.

It's not easy to pave a new path. Most people prefer to walk the old worn path. The path everyone walks on, it offers security and protection. There are no risks as there are no uncertainties but if you are willing to pave a new path so you leave a trail, then you have to be willing to be a pioneer, to go down the unknown path and get hit by a few arrows. You will then get to change your life and that of those who will follow you.

Today is the 23rd day of the year, things may not be going as planned, but remember, you have the power to change your direction. Start today.

DAY 24

"I imagine tomorrow but I plan for today."

Rudolph Mensah, Author & Speaker.

Tomorrow is a mystical land where 99% of all human aspirations and ambitions are buried. For me, there is nothing like tomorrow because when it comes we call it today. No one is guaranteed tomorrow. There is no guarantee you are going to show up tomorrow so plan your work for today.
We are here today, we are gone today. The only way to have a better tomorrow is to do your best work today.
Don't waste your time worrying about what is going to happen tomorrow. Let me tell you what is going to happen tomorrow, if you don't do your best today, tomorrow wouldn't be any different from today.

So, I plan for today and put in my best work. When tomorrow comes, my future self will thank me for what I did today but I am not worried about the events of tomorrow.

There is nothing like tomorrow. As you step out today, be your best and tomorrow will take care of itself.

DAY 25

"You are never too old to set another goal or to dream a new dream."

Les Brown; Author & Motivational Speaker.

Les is one of my favorite motivational speakers. He has had so much impact on me I would give anything to meet him just to let him know he lived a life full of global impact. I hope the universe grants me the opportunity. His story is an interesting one. You should read about him if you don't know him already.

Think of KFC and think of Cornell. There is nothing like you are old. Dreams keep us alive and young at heart. The one at 25 with no dreams is dead to life. The one at 52 with dreams is just getting started.

Your age is not the problem, your mindset is and if you have dreams, you are never old.

So, keep dreaming for there is nothing like you are too old or you are too young. Dream. Dream big.

DAY 26

> "Your imagination is your preview of life's coming attractions."

Albert Einstein; Theoretical Physicist, Nobel Prize Winner.

I have survived a lot of hard times because of my imagination. I see my glorious future, my social contribution and the impact I want to make. I imagine them all.

This book you have in your hands or on your device was first in my imagination. I have often thought about having a book I can pick up every morning, read a page and go out there full of inspiration to begin my day. When I didn't find anything like this one, I created it. Imagine, let you mind run wild.

Don't let today's pain blind you from what's coming. Hold on and tap into your imagination. The sun will surely rise and after the heavy rain, we shall stand again only to gain.

What are you looking forward to in life? Use your imagination to see it and hold on to it while you work towards it.

DAY 27

"Doubt is a killer. You just have to know who
you are and what you stand for."

Jennifer Lopez; Singer.

Someone once said "doubt kills many dreams than failure ever will".

I couldn't agree more with that. We often doubt ourselves because of our past experiences, where we come from and what we have been through.

We tried before and failed. We have seen others fail at it. Our parents couldn't succeed. No one from our tribe, race or country every succeeded so we doubt we can do it. We are also often doubted by others and we allow their doubt to overshadow our self-belief into thinking we can't do it.

One way to overcome doubt is to know yourself more than anyone. Define your life and what you stand for, this will ensure that other people can't project their fears and doubt unto you and cripple you from pursuing your dreams. No one knows enough to be a pessimist.

Let me tell you this again, I know a lot of people have told you and you have read it a hundred times, I will say it again; **"you can do it!"**.

DAY 28

"The consequences of today are determined by the actions of the past. To change your future, alter your decisions today."

Unknown

Our tomorrow depends on what we do today. You are here today because you made an appointment to be here and where you will be in a year will be determined by what you do today.

Today, decide that you will be committed to your goals. You will keep interested in your own dreams and you will dedicate the time and energy to work on them. Your future self will thank you for that.

Did you think about where you wanted to be ten years ago? What was your vision for ten years?
I don't remember if I had any, well, I was a teenager and I didn't know what I know today, but now that I know what I know today, I know exactly where I want to be the next 5, 10 and 20 years.

Every decision or action I take is geared towards the direction of my vision. Be reminded, you have the power to create your vision for the future and work towards it starting today.

DAY 29

"Hold your head and your standards high
even as people or circumstances try to pull you
down."

Tory Johnson; Author.

You will never be short of people who will make it their business to pull you down, test you and push you to the wall. Your principles, your values will be tested and how high you uphold your standards will determine whether you can withstand or give in.

It is easy to compromise these days because we have set our standards low and our values are on sale for the right price. Sometimes, we may not even hesitate to lower the price in order to get what we seek.

When you encounter failure and you will, hold your head high. When things don't go as planned, don't compromise, don't take shortcuts and don't lower your standards just to be accepted.

The best part about becoming successful is being able to look yourself in the mirror at the end of the day knowing you didn't cheat, you didn't steal, others didn't have to go down for you to rise. In order to get that satisfaction, keep your values and your standards high even as you go out today.

DAY 30

"And in the end, it's not the years in your life that count. It's the life in your years."

Abraham Lincoln; 16th U.S President.

It is not how long you live but how well you live. A man in the Bible called Methuselah lived for 969 years and all that we know about him was that "he had kids and died". Several people in the Bible got a lengthy history written about them, they lived relatively shorter lives.

Longevity doesn't determine our relevance as individuals but our contribution to humanity. We should be ashamed to die until we have contributed something to humanity.

Step out today and do something to put life into your day. It doesn't matter how the day goes if you can get home in the night and be proud you contributed to making someone's life better then you have done well. You have made the world better no matter how small contribution it was. That's the essence of life.

DAY 31

"When one door closes, another opens; but we often look so long and so regretfully upon the closed door that we do not see the one which has opened for us."

Alexander Graham Bell; Scientist.

Life is full of disappointments and how we handle them define how well we live. Now, do we dwell on the setbacks and forget to live? No.

For they say everything happens for a reason and even though we may not understand why at the moment when it does happen, we surely will get the meaning the later.

I, however, believe that things can happen without a reason but every one of us has to find his or her reason. You can always choose to find the positives even in a negative situation.

As Steve Jobs said, "we can't connect the dots looking forward we can only connect the dots looking backwards." When we look back we will understand why we needed to go through that particular situation.

When the disappointments come and they will come, don't dwell on them, move on. Another door will open right before you.

FEBRUARY

We are into the second month of the year.
Let's do a recap, what have we finished so far
and what have we started?

It is important to measure our progress and
take steps to accomplish our goals.

Maybe the first month hasn't been a smooth
ride but we have enough time to steer our boat
in the right direction.

Keep the faith, let's keep riding.

DAY 1

"Your time is limited, so don't waste it living someone else's life. Don't be trapped by dogma — which is living with the results of others people's thinking. Don't let the noise of others' opinions drown out your own inner voice. And most importantly, have the courage to follow your heart and intuition. They somehow already know what you truly want to become. Everything else is secondary."

Steve Jobs; Entrepreneur, Inventor & Industrial designer.

Other people's opinions shouldn't be your benchmark. Some people walk around always worried about what other people think of them.
You can't get anything done if all you are worried about is what people think of you.

People will talk anyway, why worry about what people will say? Everyone has an opinion about how you should live your life, human beings have a way of imposing their ideas and beliefs on others. If you don't have your personal convictions and beliefs in what you do, you are likely to be driven by what other people say.

Just meditate on Steve's words. Think deeply about them. Follow your instinct.

DAY 2

"I learned a long time ago that there is
something worse than missing the goal, and
that's not pulling the trigger."

Mia Hamm; Soccer player.

Until there is commitment, there is always bound to be
hesitancy and ineffectiveness. We have dreams, we have goals
but sometimes we are not fully committed. We don't really
want to succeed, we are only wishing.

When we are supposed to dive in we hold back, when we are
supposed to move forward, we linger behind.

We are afraid of what might go wrong so we never take action.
In the end, we only regret our inaction and that's far worse
than failure. I would rather try and fail than to ask "what if?"

The pain of regret is not something we should live with, don't
let the fear of failure hold you back from attempting and going
after your goal. When you miss, you will learn, you can try
again.

Try and fail but don't fail to try. Don't wait any longer, it's
time to pull the trigger.

DAY 3

"Owning our story can be hard but not nearly as difficult as spending our lives running from it."

Dr. Brene Brown; Research Professor.

We are all in the process. We all have something in our past we are afraid of. Like I said earlier, there is a scene in our lives which if played on the screen right now will push us to cover our faces in utter shame.

But we cannot run away from our past. It's a story, it happened, yes, but you are not a slave to it.

I recommend you read Brene's book, RISING STRONG on owning our story, dealing with our vulnerability and harnessing the power of it.

Don't allow your past story to prevent you from going into your future story.

What is ahead is better than what happened in the past, move on, you can never run away from it. Own it.

I watched the (animation) movie, THE LION KING as a kid and it tells a fascinating story which exemplifies owning our story however hard it is instead of running away from it.

You are not what happened to you, you are what you make of it.

DAY 4

"There's no next time. It's now or never."

Celestine Chua; Trainer & Life Coach.

We miss opportunities because we think we will have another chance. Life sometimes offers us another chance but what we miss we will always miss. You will never know what could have happened?

You can't count on next time. There is no guarantee you are going to show up tomorrow.

So, don't say you will wait for another chance tomorrow. Do what you have to do now, you may never get a next time.

If you live with this consciousness then you will miss less chances and be better prepared to take advantages the second chances life offers.

DAY 5

"The only disability in life is a bad attitude."

Scot Hamilton; Figure Skater & Olympic Medalist.

A bad attitude is in fact like a flat tyre, you are going nowhere until you take it off.
Your character, your manners, the way you speak, the way you approach your work, these things determine where your life goes.

Attitude comprises beliefs and values which determine how we respond to situations. Like Zig Ziglar said, "it's your attitude not your aptitude which determines your altitude" in life.
You could be intelligent, smart, beautiful, have great talents but if you have a bad attitude, you have a great disability which will make it impossible to reach your dream.

The person with no sight is not the one with a disability but the one who doesn't know how to talk with people and so ends up destroying every relationship he or she ever gets in. That's a disability.

DAY 6

"Don't rush to the arena, take your time to
train, everyone wants to play the game,
champions love to practice and then stay ready
for the time to strike."

Rudolph Mensah; Author & Speaker.

I believe so much in practice. I think it is the highest proof of
faith. Getting ready for something you haven't seen yet. You
want to compete at the next Olympics so you start practicing
today.
No one else sees you competing at the Olympics, friends and
family may not see, people around you can't see you at the
Olympics but you see yourself there so you are putting in the
work to get there.

It is important to be patient with yourself, practice takes time
and many want to get into the game right away. No, you need
to put in 200% of practice and when you think you are ready,
put in 100% more, then you are finally ready.

Listen, I don't mean practice and practice without ever giving
it a shot. No, out of fear, some people keep practicing and
marking time. This is about preparing yourself, putting in
more than it's required of you so that when you get into the
game, you can give more after you have given 100%.
Why? Because in a game, the one who can give more after he
has given his all is the one who wins. That's how we win in
life, too.

DAY 7

"What lies behind us and what lies before us
are tiny matters compared to what lies within
us"

Ralph Waldo Emerson; Essayist, Lecturer &
Poet

The kingdom of God is within us, every one of us. The power
we carry inside is more than we can ever imagine. If only we
will go into ourselves and dig up our own potential it will
amaze us all.

Today, let nothing limit you. You are more than able to
accomplish more. Rise above every limitation out there.

Every fruit carries inside it all the seeds it will ever need to
build a forest. It only has to release the seeds inside it for them
to fall down into the ground and germinate.

The process of germination is difficult. The seed has to lie
down alone in the soil, it may look dead but at the right time it
shall surely germinate.

As humans, we also need to look inside us and bring out seeds
of greatness and talents that we all have. Put them to work and
they shall surely germinate and grow into something big.

You can be more so dream more and give yourself the
opportunity to pursue your big dreams. Don't limit yourself
today.

DAY 8

"Where you were born doesn't determine where you live, how you were born doesn't determine how you live-you decide so decide!"

Rudolph Mensah; Author & Speaker.

It all comes down to what you decide to do. Never let anything hold you down. It is on you. Decide today. Your history doesn't determine your future.
You see, where you were born was only a geographical location, it has no bearing on where you can go. We are all citizens of the earth and you can go anywhere you want.

You didn't have control on how you grow up, now that you are old, you have the power to decide how the rest of your life will be. Will the next twenty years be like the last twenty years?

Making a decision isn't something we easily do but we have to make decisions all the time. Decide the kind of life you want and go after it.

DAY 9

"Don't put off living to next week, next month, next year or next decade. The only time you're ever living is in this moment."

Celestine Chua; Trainer & Life Coach.

I don't trust tomorrow. Today, right now, this very moment is the time you have to do something about your life.

John Maxwell in his book TODAY MATTERS talks a lot about making the best out of today. I would recommend you read it.

The realization of time as a commodity we have no control over will push us to be very conscious about how we use our time. We will make every second count, we will put every minute to good use and we will make sure every hour becomes productive.

As you step out, remember, all you have is today, this hour, this very minute and right now. What are you going to do?

DAY 10

"Don't go around saying the world owes you a living. The world owes you nothing. It was here first."

Mark Twain; Writer, Humourist & Lecturer.

We should all be ashamed to die until we have contributed something to humanity.

We are all here with something to make the world a better place, don't die with yours. There is so much sense of entitlement but little of responsibility among this generation.

I am sure Mark Twain would have had much to say if he was to be alive in our time. We are all asking for things to be given us but we will never lift a finger to do anything. Somehow, we have the right to everything but have no responsibility to do anything.

Today, don't ask what others can do for you, ask what you can do for others to make the world a better place?

DAY 11

"My life is my message."

Gandhi; Indian Activist.

Ours should be too. What we do, how people see us should align with our values. We should be the change we preach in the world. Others can see us and emulate our good deeds.

An old man once said, "old people love to give advice because it saves them the trouble of being a good example". It's funny but that's how many people live their lives.
They like to talk but never do. We should be disciples of our message. Walk our talk and live the way we talk.

As you walk out today, realize that someone is watching you and your life should be your message.

DAY 12

"Life is not a dress rehearsal, this is the real
show, you are on set, get ready and give it your
best shot before the curtains are pulled down,
the stage is yours, live your life before your
scene is over."

Rudolph Mensah; Author & Speaker.

The time to be serious is today. We are already getting into the
year. There is no more time to procrastinate. Resolve to be
productive.

Finishing a project is one thing successful people do. Make up
your mind to finish anything you start. When you get the taste
of finishing, it prepares you to finish everything you start.

Stop waiting for a sign to start, just start. This is it, give it your
best shot. If you are looking for a sign, read this sentence out
loud. Good, this is the time to do it.
Go out today with the determination to do your best and
become your best. This is your scene, be the lead in your own
life.

DAY 13

"Honesty is the first chapter in the book of wisdom."

Unknown

If you are honest, nothing else matters, if you are not, nothing else matters. Even in the little things, resolve to be honest today, at the workplace, with your colleagues, in school.

We often feel certain places or situations don't require our honesty. We can be honest with our Boss but not the with cab driver. We can be honest with our spouse but not with our children.

The truth has a powerful way of liberating us. Resolve to let the truth rule in all your affairs. You tell a lie, you tell another lie to cover up, soon, you will be buried under a heap of lies and you lose your integrity.

You can't even trust yourself again.

Be honest with yourself and with others.

DAY 14

"No matter how difficult and painful it may be, nothing sounds as good to the soul as the truth."

Martha Beck; Author.

I don't know how many times you have heard this but I will reiterate what the Bible says, "you shall know the truth and the truth shall set you free".

There is nothing liberating like the knowledge of the truth. No matter how hard it gets, never allow lies and dishonesty to taint your life and values.

As we read yesterday, honesty is a powerful tool in liberating us and giving us the freedom and happiness we seek in life.

In all your dealings, resolve to uphold the truth and nothing but the truth.

DAY 15

"Your work is to discover your work and then,
with all your heart, to give yourself to it."

Buddha; Spiritual Teacher.

There are two primary focuses in life, one is to discover why we are here and two is to go out there and do everything to make it happen.

Today, everything you do should be about becoming what you dream of. It is your work to devote yourself to finding yourself and becoming your best self.

So many of us keep marking time afraid to go out there and work on the dream we have, the ideas we have. You don't need anyone's permission to begin, if you have found something which gives your life meaning, go out there and do it.

If you haven't found it yet, keep looking till you find it, and even as you look, do something every day. You don't have to wait, just work on what you have, where you are and soon you will realize that the thing which seems insignificant will lead you to your purpose.

Work on it as if your life depends on it because it does.

DAY 16

"One person with a belief is equal to a force of 99 who have only interests."

John Stuart Mill; Philosopher.

Don't look for the many to get things done, look for dedication and commitment. Whether it is team building or getting the needed support for a project. Look out for enthusiasm not passive interest.

You don't need cheerleaders to succeed. You don't need support groups all the time, all you need are the right people with the right energy to propel you to your dream because they themselves are on a journey to becoming great.

Identify with the right kind of people. You can't hang around negative people and expect to get positive results in life.

Sometimes, it takes only one person to believe in you, to support you and to help you. That's all you need today. Don't look for numbers. Look for someone who believes in you and your ideas.

DAY 17

"Everyone has his own specific vocation or mission in life…Therein he cannot be replaced, nor can his life be repeated. Thus, everyone's task is as unique as is his specific opportunity to implement it."

Viktor Frankl; Neurologist.

You are you and you are unique so is everyone else. The only problem is that many are yet to recognize it and live as such. Remember that as you step out today.

This means that we all have the responsibility of finding our purpose and living it. Our failure to do that robs the world of our talent and our contribution. Therefore, it is not only important that you find your life work it is also necessary that you devote yourself to living it.

Meditate on it. Write down your thoughts at the end of the day what your unique mission or vocation is and how you are going to live it. It's your responsibility.

DAY 18

"Here is the test to find whether your mission
on earth is finished. If you're alive, it isn't."

Richard Bach; Writer.

You are alive today, if you are reading this then it surely means
you are alive. You can read, you can do a lot of things most
people can't, especially dead people.

We often overlook the gift of life and focus so much on what
we don't have. The fact that you are alive is enough proof that
you can become what you dream of. It means you have the
chance of giving it another shot.
You can correct your mistakes, you can try again, you can
work harder. Most importantly the rest of your life could be
different from the past because you have the opportunity to
chart a new course for your life.

It's not over yet.

DAY 19

"It is never too late to be what you might have been."

George Eliot; Novelist.

Never limit what you can do because of your age, you are never too young or old to do anything. It is a matter of will and determination.

The world is full of people who fulfilled their life long ambitions at an old age, I won't give you stories upon stories of such people and I am sure you know a number of them.

Age they say is just a number. Listen, what matters is your belief, determination and commitment to change the direction of your life.

Stop brooding over the past and what could have happened, go out there today and start what you should have started yesterday.

DAY 20

"Done is better than perfect."

Sheryl Sandberg; Chief Operating Officer of Facebook.

Many are at a standstill because they want to be perfect from the beginning. They want to be loved by everyone and be liked by all. This was my problem when I began writing. I was always worried about how perfect my work is. Getting things done is better than waiting to be perfect.

That is progress and that's what you should strive for. Every master you see has been an amateur before. Every one you see who is good at what he does today was poor at doing it yesterday.

Do I stop writing because my first four books haven't gone on to become New York Times bestsellers? No. of course not, if I have to write 1,000 books to have my books all over the world, that's what I am going to do and I know that with every book I write, I am getting better at my craft.

Soon, people will wonder how I became so good. I am simply getting things done. Getting things done brings a sense of fulfilment and accomplishment. It gives you confidence to tackle other projects. Finishing my first book was the impetus for me to keep going on to become an Amazon bestselling author.

Get things done, don't worry about being perfect.

DAY 21

"Remembering you are going to die is the best way I know to avoid the trap of thinking you have something to lose. You are already naked. There is no reason not to follow your heart."

Steve Jobs; Entrepreneur, Inventor & Industrial designer.

This is my morning reminder every day. It should be yours too. Again, we are not guaranteed we are going to show up tomorrow.

Someone said, the day you were born you were old enough to die. Every day you live is an opportunity to do what you are here for. Don't be trapped into thinking you have something to lose for trying and failing, you are already naked.

You lose nothing. You only lose by refusing to work on your ideas and dreams.

Live your life, today, right now.

DAY 22

"Do what you love and the money will follow."

Marsha Sinetar; Author.

Many have advised and so whether you will take it or not, is your decision. I believe this is true.

When your focus is on helping people with whatever you are doing, you will surely be rewarded with money for what you do.

I don't know how many times you have heard this, but hear me, it's true. Money is a reward for solving a problem.
If I asked you to give me $2 because I am facing a challenging situation, you will find that odd to do especially if we have no relationship and it's not a charity work.

You would rather give me the $2 when I have given you something of value, like this book. You see, the world is full of needs, every need you solve will bring people who will be willing to exchange money for the solution you have provided.

Provide value, the money will come.

DAY 23

"The more I want to get something done, the less I call it work."

Richard Bach; Writer.

Just like Thomas Edison said, "he never worked a day in his life, it was all fun". When you do what you love and love what you do, then it is not much of what we call work. Today, infuse love into whatever you are doing and be enthused about finishing it. You will love it. Every step of the way. When we grumble and whine about everything we do, we never put in our best.

Do it happy. Do it with enthusiasm, do it with passion. Today. Be happy. You may not be doing what you love right now, but you can love what you do till you can do what you love.

It's your attitude which will either make you happy or miserable.

DAY 24

"Don't ask yourself what the world needs, ask yourself what makes you come alive. And then go and do that. Because what the world needs is people who are alive."

Howard Thurman; Author, Philosopher & Theologian

What makes you come alive? This is something we must all think about. Some love painting, some are excited with great writings, others play sports, others are good at leading, there are those who are good at their craft.

This is for your meditating. I don't want to mar the waters with my commentary.

Answer the question, "what makes you come alive?"

Be alive, stay alive and make the world better.

DAY 25

"What you do makes a difference, and you have to decide what kind of difference you want to make."

Jane Goodall; Primatologist & Anthropologist.

Someone once told me "everyone is an example, you however decide what type of example you want to be, a good one or a bad one.

How do you want people to remember you? How do you want people to feel after interacting with you? Make the conscious effort today to determine what kind of example you want to be to people.

Have this in mind and make sure everything you do is fashioned towards making this difference.

What kind of difference do you want to make?

DAY 26

"If you have built castles in the air, your work need not be lost; that is where they should be. Now put foundations under them."

Henry David Thoreau; Essayist, Poet & Philosopher.

You can have beautiful dreams which may seem unattainable but don't let that distract you. Take a step back and ask yourself, what can I do to get what I have dreamed of?
You are allowed to build a prototype of your dream, see the big picture in your mind and don't be discouraged, begin to work towards it.

Begin from the bottom and build your dream up. So, don't dream small dreams, dream big dreams and then be ready to put in the work.

Let's go out there today and work on our foundation while holding on the vision.

DAY 27

"No matter where you are in life right now, no matter who you are, no matter how old you are – it is never too late to be who you are meant to be."

Esther & Jerry Hicks; Couple, Authors & Inspirational Speakers.

I want you to repeat this to yourself throughout the day. Sometimes we allow current circumstances to dictate the direction of our lives. we believe that because we may be going through a rough patch in our lives right now, we can't possibly do what we want to do.

We may not have the money or the support but all you have to do is focus on yourself and what you have on the inside.

Remind yourself every hour that you have the power to become what you are meant to be. With this belief and commitment, you have every power to live the life you envision.

Never think it's too late to do anything. Believe!

DAY 28

"Don't be afraid of the space between your dreams and reality. If you can dream it, you can make it so."

Belva Davis; Journalist.

Many of us are afraid of how long it will take to become what we dream of. We consider how long we have to be in school to get a degree, to get a masters' degree or to obtain a PhD.

We consider how long we have to work to attain success, how long we have to save to accumulate the money we want, the space between our dream and reality scares us and stops us in our tracks.

My mentor once asked; the time will pass anyway so what would you rather be doing?

The time will pass, what we do with it is what is important. You may say if it will take seven years to attain your dream, you won't do it, but what else will you be doing with the seven years?

Start now and start early.

MARCH

It's the third month of the year. This is the last month of the first quarter of the year. We should be making some good progress. But hey, don't judge your progress with other people's progress but by your own potential.

This is not time to be finding excuses. Let's keep running.

DAY 1

"No great thing is created suddenly."

Epictetus; Philosopher.

There is nothing like overnight success. It usually takes ten to fifteen years to become an overnight success. You have to keep working on that dream of yours.
If it is something small you are working on, you can get it done in a month but if you are looking to build a lasting legacy, establish something great, it won't happen suddenly.

You must be willing to put in the work required to become great. It doesn't happen by spontaneous combustion, you have to set yourself on fire and fan your flame gradually. Continue to seek people who can help you fan your flame.

Enjoy the process. Enjoy the journey of investing your whole life into worthwhile dream.

It won't happen immediately but definitely if you don't quit.

DAY 2

"In life, as in football, you won't go far unless
you know where the goalposts are."

Arnold H. Glasgow; Businessman and
Humourist.

We can't talk about goal settings any more than we know
already. It will only become monotonous. I believe we have
heard or read countless number of times why we need to set
goals for our lives. I have written a book on it.

Having a goal in life brings focus and a sense of direction to
our lives. We just don't drift along. We know what we want
and where we are going. Without goals we are just a
wondering generality as Zig Ziglar describes it.

If you are looking to set and achieve SMARTER GOALS, get
my book on SETTING AND ACHIEVING SMARTER
GOALS EVERY TIME! On my amazon page. Find link in
the closing pages.

DAY 3

"When we are motivated by goals that have
deep meaning, by dreams that need
completion, by pure love that needs
expressing, then we truly live life."

Greg Anderson; Personal Trainer.

Allow this quote to sink into your mind. Meditate on it.

When it comes to goal setting, we will have a hard time accomplishing them if we only set goals as a means of achieving or reaching a specific target without any deeper meaning for our lives, it may not be a worthwhile goal. I explain this in my book.

A goal when accomplished should mean something deeper than just getting what you want. It should be for the greater good of humanity. Why do you want to become a doctor not I want to become a doctor? When we tie our goals to just becoming without a deeper meaning of why we want what we want, goals have no meaning to our lives and those around us.

How will accomplishing your goal contribute to the good of humanity? How much love do you want to express? Life has more meaning when we live to express love and make dreams come true giving meaning not to us alone but to people around us.

DAY 4

"The most important thing about goals is having one."

Geoffrey F. Abert; Author.

That sounds quite simple because it is, when we develop goals for our life, we have direction for our lives. when we don't have goals for our lives, we have no sense of direction so the most important thing about goals is basically having one.
Just have a goal. That's all. Life without goals is like walking in the dark.

You can't simply drag yourself through life not knowing the direction you are heading. You need to establish a direction for every aspect of your life.
Career development, where do you see yourself in ten years. Your relationship or marriage, what do you want to see in your partner and how do you want to raise your children? How are you going to contribute to a successful relationship?

Your health, your finances, your spiritual development, what are your goals? You see, going through life hoping for the best, just wishing is one of the worst plans you can ever have. Decide exactly what you want, write it down and work on it. What's your life goal?

DAY 5

"The trouble with not having a goal is that you can spend your life running up and down the field and never score."

Bill Copeland; Poet, Writer & Historian.

Wait. Don't skip it yet. Yes, we are still talking about goals. Set goals for every aspect of your life; professional, career, health, relationship, financial and personal development.

Find Brian Tracy's videos on YouTube about setting goals and get to work. They were very instrumental in helping me set goals for my life when I was starting out.

It is true that many are spending their lives running up and down the field not knowing exactly where they are going.

Don't skip it today, pick a pen and paper, begin to set goals for your life. Don't postpone it, do it today.

DAY 6

"If you don't design your own life plan,
chances are you'll fall into someone else's
plan. And guess what they have planned for
you? Not much."

Jim Rohn; Entrepreneur, Author &
Motivational Speaker.

This is why you need to set your own smarter goals. Yes, you need to set goals for yourself. Don't fall into someone else's plans. I have intentionally chosen to keep talking about goal settings until you get the concept if you haven't already.

Think about it. For every aspect of your life, again, set goals. Spiritual, career and professional life, marriage and relationships, etc.

People say if you don't work on your dreams you will be helping others work on theirs for the rest of your life. You may be working for someone, you should still have a plan on how long you will be employed and when you will be advancing in your career or building your own.
Get to work, design your own life plan.

DAY 7

"Everything is always created twice, first in
the mind and then in reality."

Stephen Covey; Educator, Author &
Businessman.

I believe this. Really, I do believe this. I had seen this book finished even before I started writing. If you can't see it in your mind, you can't get it in your hands.

Imagination is a powerful tool God has given us. Use it. Instead of worrying, use your mind to imagine.

This is what the law of attraction teaches but I am more concerned about taking action after imagining. But it begins with you imagining what exactly you want.

Remember, if you can't see it in your mind, you can't hold it in your hands.

DAY 8

"You need a plan to build a house. To build a life, it is even more important to have a plan or goal."

Zig Ziglar; Author, Salesman and Motivational Speaker.

Do you have a plan for your life for the next five, ten and twenty years?

If not, get to work right away. No kidding, you really need a plan for your life spanning five, ten and twenty years.
We are where we are now because five, ten and twenty years ago we didn't actually plan how we wanted our lives to be 20 years later.
I am assuming a lot of young people are reading.

The next twenty years of our lives will change based on the plan we put in place today. Planning is one of the hardest things we do which makes our lives easier.
Plan your life, don't live without a roadmap of where you want to go. You get lost easily without a plan. A plan doesn't have to be exact, it should however give us a sense of direction.

DAY 9

"The tragedy of life doesn't lie in not reaching your goal. The tragedy lies in having no goals to reach."

Benjamin Mays; Baptist Minister & Civil Right Leader.

I am actually not letting you off the hook until you set your life goals. I have come to realize that it's easy to just go through life without a plan which is why most people fail in life. I don't want you to fail.

Without goals, you have no direction in life. You live as the days come and go.

If you live your life without any direction (goals), you are likely to end up anywhere. You don't want to end up anywhere, you want to end up where you'll be happy. To do that successfully, you need to set goals.

You should make sure you set goals for short and long-term. This is not a prediction of how your life will turn out but it is a map which will direct your path towards the future you want.

DAY 10

"People with clear, written goals, accomplish
far more in a shorter period of time than
people without them could ever imagine."

Unknown

One important thing about setting and accomplishing your
goals is writing them down. Don't just keep it in your mind,
scribble it.

When you write it down, in your own handwriting it forces
you to act. There is a powerful force behind that I can't
possibly explain.

Pick up your journal or diary and write down your goals in
black ink. Yes, do that today and read it every day.

Have all your goals in one place, refer to them throughout the
day. Read them when you seem lost, read it again and again,
remind yourself of your goals while you pursue them.

"When your goals are clear you will come up with the exactly
the right answer to achieve your goals at exactly the right time"
– Brian Tracy

DAY 11

"In order to be irreplaceable, one must always
be different."

Coco Chanel; Fashion Designer.

We are often afraid of what makes us different forgetting
that's also what makes us unique.

We can't simply follow the norm and expect to be any
different from the many other ordinary people.

The world is full of ordinary people, if you want to be
extraordinary you have to be willing to do the extra work
required to be different.

What makes you different then? What are your super powers?
What are you good at? Develop and enhance the things you
are good at and become great at them.

Be known for it, be great at it, let them call you when it needs
to be done, if you are doing what everyone else is doing, you
can easily be replaced.

DAY 12

"You are not given a pen and paper to write your life history at the end of your life, you start writing when you start your life, just so you don't forget, and you are writing your history now as you're reading this. What's your legacy so far?"

Rudolph Mensah, Author & Speaker

Most people forget that what we are now is a result of tiny decisions we have made along the way. You are where you are because of the millions of tiny decisions you made in the past.

You are where you are right now because you decided to be here knowingly or unknowingly. The moment you wake up, you start making decisions, even before that, you must decide what time to wake up, what to do and how to prepare for the day. These daily decisions compound into how our day goes and the kind of life we live and the history we leave behind.

Your life is your decision, every day, you determine the course of your life, don't forget that. Make sure you write a good page today.

DAY 13

"There are no secrets to success. It is the result of preparation, hard work, learning from failure."

Colin Powell; Former U.S. National Security Advisor.

Well, there are no secrets. As Colin says, to get what you want, you have to prepare for it. Preparation separates unsuccessful people with talent from those who succeed.

This requires hard work, there is no way around hard work and once you are trying, you may fail. Deal with it, learn from it and get better. This is how you succeed.

I talk more about this in my book **Becoming Your Dream** and a lot of personal development books I have read do also.

Over the years, it has become increasingly clear that there are no secrets, you may have what it takes to succeed but the question is, are you willing to give all it takes to succeed?

DAY 14

"Take criticism seriously, but not personally.
If there is truth or merit in the criticism, try to
learn from it. Otherwise, let it roll right off
you."

Hillary Clinton; Politician & Former First
Lady of the U.S.

Coming from someone like Hillary, let's not go to whether you like her or not, I believe she has had lots of criticism as a politician and therefore her advice is sound.

Don't let criticism go to your heart and don't let praise go to your head. Know how to handle them. Control your emotions. Learn from your mistakes but never be kept down by others opinion.

If they don't know you personally, don't take it personal. It is common for people to talk about you even without ever meeting you personally. Gossip goes around and people carry it along without the need to verify.

When others criticize you, ask yourself if what they are talking about is true or otherwise. If it's true, pay attention to it, commit to changing from it for the better. If it's otherwise then don't let it bother you, let it roll off you.

DAY 15

"You cannot live your life to please others.
The choice must be yours."

White Queen; from Alice in Wonderland.

Trapped into thinking everyone must like you? I am sorry to disappoint you but not everyone will like you.

I have said that this was one truth which took me a long time to grasp. I always tried to be in the good books of everyone. I tried not to offend anyone, I tiptoed around people.
Until I read a quote which said, "I don't know the secret of success I know the secret of failure, trying to please everyone." You are imprisoning yourself if you think you can make every human being happy.

My mum told me you can lie down for people to walk on you and they will still complain you are not flat enough. My grandma told me, you could be a juicy ripe mango and someone who has been eating mangoes all his life will say, "I don't like mangoes" just because it's you.
Don't seek approval from people to blossom, just go ahead and live your life, those who are meant to be in it will find a way to be in it. The universe will always ensure that.

DAY 16

"It is your attitude, not your aptitude, that
determines your altitude."

Zig Ziglar; Author, Salesman and Motivational
Speaker.

Attitude is a very important determining factor in becoming successful. How you deal with people, how you relate to your superiors, colleagues and subordinates all depend on your attitude.

People will determine how far you go and your attitude determines how well you get on with people.

Building a good and solid attitude takes time. You will be tested, you will encounter times when your attitude will be tried, when others try to make you lower your attitude, hold on to your standards.

As you step out today, determine to have a good attitude towards all manner of persons.

DAY 17

"Logic will get you from A to B. Imagination
will take you everywhere."

Albert Einstein; Theoretical Physicist & Nobel
Prize Winner.

We've talked about imagination, already right? Yeah. Don't forget how powerful your imagination is and can be.

Einstein, one of the most brilliant minds of the time elaborates on the importance of our imagination. If we can tap into the limitless power of our imagination, nothing will be impossible in our lives.

Don't be limited with logic, allow your imagination to run wild today and come up with every crazy idea possible.

Logic looks for reasons, numbers, fact, data which is great but these things limit you. You can't go beyond what the numbers say, you can't dream beyond what logic concludes on as possible or impossible, the only time you can do more than what's on paper is when you tap into the power of your imagination.
If you are looking to access the infinite possibilities of your mind, tap into your imagination today.

DAY 18

"Every day is an opportunity for us to write a new chapter in our life story, we don't allow what happened yesterday to affect what we can do today. Today, is not a continuation of yesterday, you have a brand-new piece of paper, you have the power to change the narrative. What are you writing?"

Rudolph Mensah, Author & Speaker

Perhaps, things haven't gone as planned so far. The year hasn't been good as you imagined.

You can always learn your lessons and chart a new path for the future. You are never out of options, you are only out of options when you stop looking.

You have the opportunity to begin anew today. The universe has granted you a new day, God has given you breath for today. You are here, it doesn't matter what happened yesterday. It doesn't matter who did what to you and when and how painful it was. All that is in the past, you are alive today, you have the power to change how the story ends.

What are you going to do with a brand-new day? A 24-hour opportunity to write a magnificent chapter of your life. Get to work on your chapter today with enthusiasm.

DAY 19

"All children are artists. The problem is how
to remain an artist once he grows up."

Pablo Picasso; Prolific Artist.

Children have no boundaries to their imaginations because
there is no logic to their thinking.

They are yet to be introduced to the tax rates, the percentage
of new businesses failing, how hard it is to jump, how difficult
it is to draw, to paint, to sing, etc. Only adults have the
experience of logical reasoning.

As we grow and we learn facts, it begins to restrict our
creativity and ability to dream, to try and make mistakes.
Creativity only means you are not afraid of making mistakes.
Ken Robinson once said, "if you afraid of making mistakes
then you can never do anything original."

This is not only about artists but every area of our lives. As we
grow we think more than we use our instinct. We will be at
our best if we can marry our instinct with our intellect.

We need to rediscover what it is to be a child, to have no fear
of failing, of trying and of dreaming and being creative.

DAY 20

"Learn from the mistakes of others. You can't live long enough to make them all yourself."

Eleanor Roosevelt; Politician, Diplomat, Activist & Former First Lady of the U.S.

A wise man will learn from one rebuke than a fool will ever learn from a thousand rebukes, paraphrased from the book of Proverbs in the Bible.

You can learn by making mistakes yourself, what they call learning from experience. Wisdom will teach you to understand that you don't have to make all the mistakes yourself.

You can learn from others mistakes. Apart from not living long enough to make every mistake yourself, it saves you time and energy you can invest into other things.

In this era where people put their experiences into books and other formats, the wise thing to do is to learn from them. If it took someone fifty years to understand a concept, I would spend $15 to buy a book he wrote on it and read it in 3 hours to learn something which took him 50 years to understand.

So, as you step out today, be looking for the opportunity to learn from people who have gone ahead. They can teach you a lot.

DAY 21

"Why compare yourself with others? No one in the entire world can do a better job of being you than you."

Unknown

How many times do you want to hear this before you get out of the paradigm of comparison?

You will never be happy always comparing yourself with other people. As it says in the poem "Desiderata", "there will always be lesser and greater persons than you".

You are unique just as anyone else. You have to recognize your own uniqueness. When you do, you will realize life is only fulfilling when we do what we are meant to do.

Stop worrying about who likes you, do you like you?

DAY 22

"When you are totally at peace with yourself,
nothing can shake you."

Deepam Chatterjee; Author.

So, we talked about finding and living in your own uniqueness yesterday. This a process. You won't find it overnight. Some people find it early in life, others have to look for a while and others too will take a long time.

What you shouldn't do is to stop looking. That's life, find what makes you unique and committing the rest of your life to manifesting that uniqueness.

When you do find and live in your own uniqueness, that's when you are totally at peace with yourself. This is only when you can live a fulfilled life when nothing can shake you. So as long you as you keep looking at other people for validation, you are never at peace.

DAY 23

"If you put yourself in a position where you
have to stretch outside your comfort zone,
then you are forced to expand your
consciousness."

Unknown

Be challenged to do something you have always been afraid to
do today.

Make sure you are not in harm's way but make that call, send
the letter, write that proposal, start that business, write that
book.

You see we can't accomplish great feat because we are always
playing within the limited confines of what's possible for us.
As we described days ago, make use of your imagination.
Dream impossible dreams and see how your mind will come
up with all the solutions you never thought about.

Don't allow yourself to bail out when things get tough, put
yourself in a position where you have no choice whatsoever
than to go forward.

When I start, I close the door behind me because I don't want
an excuse to run back when things get tough.

DAY 24

"Confidence comes not from always being
right but not fearing to be wrong."

Unknown

As long as you are trying new ideas you are bound to make mistakes, to be wrong, to fail.

Often, we are restricted by the fear of making mistakes. We give up on being creative when we are held by fear of making mistakes.

When we dare to risk and take action on our dreams, we build confidence to dare greatly. Not being afraid of making mistakes releases our inner creativity.

You develop confidence from trying and failing and trying again and getting it right.

Go out today and don't be afraid of being wrong, don't be afraid of failing but be afraid of not trying.

DAY 25

"Confidence is not a guarantee of success, but
a pattern of thinking that will improve your
likelihood of success, a tenacious search for
ways to make things work."

Dr. John Elliot from Overachievement

Without confidence, you can't get anything done. Yesterday,
we talked about how confidence comes about, not by holding
on but by daring.

It develops by trying and not being afraid of losing. Again, if
you are afraid of losing then you have no right to win.

Fear and timidity never guarantee success. Any idea you have
requires that you are bold enough to try it. To take action on
your idea, it requires confidence.
This confidence doesn't mean you will succeed at the first try
but it improves your chances of winning by a 70%. The one
without confidence is already lost.

Today, you need to be confident in taking action on your
ideas. Don't let someone talk you out of it. Confidence is that
small voice inside you telling to not be afraid and to try it. Go
and do it. Be bold and confident.

DAY 26

---

*"To wish you were someone else is to waste
the person you are."*

Unknown

If you don't agree with this, then you are surely wasting your life.

You can admire other people, you can take inspiration from their lives, you can learn from them but never wish you were someone else.

Who should be you then? Bask in your own uniqueness, the world needs someone like you to be here with us. Don't photocopy others when you were born original.

If you copy others, you deny the world of your originality. The world needs the original you not the photocopied you. Be yourself, everyone else is taken, someone once said.

DAY 27

"You can be the lead in your own life."

Kerry Washington; Actress & Producer.

Exactly, Kerry is a lead actress in Shonda Rhimes' Tv Series, Scandal. I started watching some episodes of this series after reading this quote from Kerry Washington. I have always wanted to relate what people say to who they are.

That is one of the reasons why I add a profile of the people whose quotes are in this book, this will help you to better understand their nugget.

Kerry, admonishing us to be the lead in our own lives tells us more knowing she is the lead in her own life not just in movies. It's your life, you can write your script, direct it, determine how it will go and who should be in it.

You have all the power you need to control your life. Don't lease it to someone else. To dictate how your life should play out.

Be in control of your life, be the lead, don't be a supporting cast in your own life.

DAY 28

"Your worth consists in what you are and not
in what you have."

Thomas Edison; Inventor & Businessman.

No one is going to stand up at your funeral and talk about the
kind of car you had, the kind of phone you used, the house
you lived in or the degrees you had but the kind of person you
were.
Life is not about possessions but what we do and how we
make others feel. Stop making life about possessions.

Who are you? I don't mean your name or what you do. I don't
mean where you come from or your race.

Really, who are you?

Are you kind? Gentle, loves to help people, stops crying just to
wipe other people's tears, who are you?
We all have a unique ability and when we contribute this to the
world, the world becomes a better place for all of us.

Today, resolve to be a better person, kind, loving, forgiving
and patient. That is who people will remember you for not
your wrist watch or your mobile phone.

DAY 29

"Others can stop you temporarily – you are the
only one who can do it permanently."

Zig Ziglar; Author, Salesman and Motivational
Speaker.

This is truth. Don't hold yourself back. No one can hold you
back from doing what you dream of but yourself. You can do
it only when you allow yourself to do it. Don't limit what you
can do today.

There are times we allow what we cannot do to stop us from
doing what we can do. The most important thing to do is to
invest our energy into the things which bring us fulfilment.

You can stop yourself from going after your dream when you
give up. Keep working, don't let the frustrations and
disappointments stop you from pursuing your dream.

DAY 30

"We do not need magic to transform our world. We carry all of the power we need inside ourselves already."

J.K. Rowling, Novelist, Screenwriter & Producer.

Coming from someone like J. K. Rowling, I wouldn't say much in addition to it. Her famous Harry Potter books had a lot of magic in them but in the end, she is telling us we don't need magic to change the world. She didn't need magic herself to change the world, she had all the power inside her.

Each and every one of us carries a tremendous amount of power to transform our world but often we look so hard at external forces we forget we have something special inside us to tap into.

Don't look to the east, north, west or south, look inside of you for what you are searching for. You have greatness inside of you.

The only way to harness this power within us is to believe in ourselves. Don't doubt yourself, there are plenty of people to do that for us.

Go out there every day with the belief that you carry the power to change the direction of your life all by yourself.

DAY 31

"The person who says something is impossible should not interrupt the person who is doing it."

Chinese proverb

Take this advice. Seriously, don't let someone tell you to stop chasing your dream because they couldn't accomplish theirs.

Don't turn down your dream because someone else is uncomfortable with the volume. It's your dream. Make it happen.

It is therefore important to not allow people to disrupt our pursuit of purpose. Friends and family are the first group of people who will try to stop you from pursuing your dream.

Don't be interrupted, you can do it.

APRIL

Today, we begin the second quarter of the year. It's the fourth month of the year.

We need to keep focused on our goals and we shouldn't forget to enjoy the journey. We are alive, we have the gift of life. Let's make the best out of it.

DAY 1

"You can't please everyone, and you can't make everyone like you."

Katie Couric; Journalist & Author.

Not everyone will like you, the truth which took me a long time to come to terms with. I have always wanted to be everyone's guy, cool, calm, loved by all.

Why would anyone hate me or not like me? Come on, I am way too cool for you to hate me. I was kidding myself. After I published my first book, I had friends and family who suddenly didn't seem happy I was taken a new path in life, some made me feel like I am being proud and others became jealous.

Others took it upon themselves to discredit my personality and make others see me wrongly. I thought everyone would be happy for me, well, not everyone was.

When you go out to become your dream, to chase your vision, remember this, don't worry about pleasing everyone, that's a recipe for failure.

Be yourself, be your best and those who will stay with you will stick, don't make it your personal business to make everyone like you because not everyone will.

DAY 2

"Be a first-rate version of yourself, not a
second-rate version of someone else."

Judy Garland; Singer, Actress & Vaudevillian.

When you photocopy, you lose resolution, "be yourself,
everyone else is taken", someone once said. Never try to
imitate or copy other people.
There is something in you only you can bring out to this
world. I am not here to be another Les Brown or Jim Rohn.

I learn from them, I admire them, I study them but I will fail
my generation if I don't become myself but just another Jim
Rohn or another Zig Ziglar.

My only goal is to get better every day at what I do. Whether I
am taking care of patients, writing or speaking.

Always strive for progress, be better than you were yesterday.
Don't copy but you can steal other ideas, customize it for
yourself, add your own uniqueness and get better at what you
do. Never copy.

When you copy you lose resolution.

DAY 3

"Life has no limitations; except the ones you make."

Les Brown; Author & Motivational Speaker.

Obviously one of my favorite motivational speakers. Coming from such a difficult background, Les was abandoned with his twin brother in an uncompleted building and adopted by a single mother. Labelled mentally retarded, having no college education he still didn't limit himself.

Today, he is celebrated around the world. So, when Les says there are no limitations, there are no limitations.

Limitations only exist in our minds, if we can go beyond what's possible and what's impossible in our minds then we can break every physical barrier.

Today, don't limit yourself.

DAY 4

"The best years of your life are the ones in which you decide your problems are your own. You do not blame them on your mother, the ecology, or the president. You realize that you control your own destiny."

Albert Ellis; Psychologist.

Blaming never solved any problem. You can choose to blame everyone and everything and there will never be a shortage of people and circumstances to blame but in the end the problem won't go away.

You can also choose to take responsibility for your life and solve your problems. Oh, how happy you will be if you begin to take responsibility.

Go out today with the mindset that you are responsible for your life and you will work to make the rest of your life the best of your life.

DAY 5

'If you don't get out of the box you've been raised in, you won't understand how much bigger the world is."

Angelina Jolie; Actress, Filmmaker & Humanitarian.

Our view of the world is shaped by our geographical location, our interactions with other people and how many different perspectives we have of the world.

Our parents teach us their principles, beliefs and doctrines. We grow up living with them without questioning why we have to do what we do.

To become successful, you need to develop an open mind to go beyond the borders of what you think you know and seek different perspectives. Listen to others, learn their stories, find out why that other person is the way he or she is.

Stop judging, no prejudices, no misconceptions, learn, unlearn and relearn. You begin to appreciate life better when you begin to see from different perspectives.

Get rid of the box. The world is too big for your mediocrity.

DAY 6

"We are what we repeatedly do; excellence,
then, is not an act but a habit."

Aristotle; Philosopher.

We do it once, we do it again, it becomes a habit, we repeat it, we get better, we become excellent at it. It is not a onetime event but a repeated series of events. That's how we become excellent. It means you have to be willing to try, to fail, to make mistakes and to keep going again and again.

You want to excel at writing? Write every day. Write regardless of your emotional state. Whatever you intend to get better at, do it every day. Let it become a habit.

Science says that if you can do it consistently for 21 days, it will become a habit. Try it, commit to doing something small everyday continuously for 21 days and develop a positive habit.

It will change your life.

DAY 7

"Power's not given to you. You have to take it."

Beyoncé Knowles Carter; Singer & Songwriter.

It's not just power. Happiness isn't given, you can choose to be happy. Success isn't given. You earn it. Don't sit down waiting for good things to happen to you. Go out there and work on your ideas. Get busy on your dream.

No one is going to hand anything down to you. The universe doesn't hand out gifts, it rewards those who work hard for what they seek. Don't wait for some government somewhere to make it easy for you to succeed, don't rely on the state to provide everything you need, you want something, go and get it.
No one stands in your way but you. If you are expecting people to give you things, I am sorry to say, you may be waiting for a long time.

Do you want to be successful? Go out there knowing you that you have the power to make it happen.

DAY 8

"If you are born to kill an elephant, you don't go chasing after rats and get hurt in the process."

Ghanaian proverb

My father told me this proverb when I was 8. In life, there should be priorities, never be distracted by temporal gratifications which stop you from getting to the greater goal. Know what you want and go after it.

Don't get into other territories because everyone else is going there. Focus on your journey, enjoy the process and never be distracted from the big picture.

At every point in your life, ask yourself what you really want because things which seem like what you want may be presented you. Until you can clearly define what you want, you may settle for something which looks like it.
I think Robbin Sharma once said, "many people will not accomplish the all-time great because they settle for the short term good."

DAY 9

"Life is either a daring adventure, or it is nothing."

Helen Keller; Author, Political activist & Lecturer.

Either you understand this or nothing else. Either you agree with it or nothing else. Either you are willing to take some risk or you are just going to take the back seat and hope something good happens.

You won't fall if you don't climb but what joy is there if you spend your whole life on the ground?

Get out today and work on your dream and don't just be merely trying to go through the day. Live, don't just exist. We are not getting out of here alive, you can either die on the sidelines or get in the game.

DAY 10

"A successful man is one who can lay a firm foundation with the bricks others have thrown at him."

David Brinkley; Newscaster.

Yes, some people will dislike you enough that they will throw stones at you. They will ridicule you, embarrass you but how you react to the negativity will determine whether you will become successful or not. I don't have time to stop and respond to every hateful comment online.

I am moving on to greater things. Haters will keep hating, keep being great. And oh, my father always told me, "if someone hates you for no reason, give them a reason, be more awesome."
If you believe in what you are doing, keep going. You don't have time to waste on the media, the naysayers and people who don't like you.

DAY 11

"You already have every characteristic necessary for success if you recognize, claim, develop and use them"

Zig Ziglar; Author, Salesman and Motivational Speaker.

Pay attention to these words: **recognize, claim, develop and use them**, how many people know what they are actually here for and are committed to making it happen?

Read my book BECOMING YOUR DREAM for insight into recognizing your purpose and fulfilling it, learn how to DEVELOP it and then USE it. There are several other books to help you on that.

We are often not aware of what we are capable of. You have all you need to become successful, the question is, are you ready to give it your all to make it happen?

DAY 12

"The big secret in life is that there is no big secret. Whatever your goal, you can get there if you're willing to work."

Oprah Winfrey; Media Proprietor & Talk Show Host.

There is no secret. It's just that not everyone is ready and willing to put in the work required to becoming great. At this point of the book, I thought about just having a 365-quote book without any expositions from me. I have seen other people compile quotes, many of them but I have only seen a few compilations with little bit of explanation from the author.

I started this book because I wanted something different. I really want to give up right now as my back aches from writing and editing over 400 pages. It's a lot of hard work but I am doing this because it wasn't out there. As I am typing this very sentence, I want to just go back to a compilation of quotes. Which is easier but that's not what I want. That's not what you my reader deserve. I want to give you something you can pick up in the morning and read to set the tone for your day not just another quotes book.

That's the difference, it's not easy but this book will be successful (give more meaning to readers and help them have a good day) because I was willing to put in the work and make it different from all the other quotes book out there.

DAY 13

"We all start out with no discipline, no patience, no perseverance, no determination. People say, you have talent. No, the gift is to realize that we all start out even. Whether we messed up or put our best foot forward with these four qualities, we take care of our mental, physical and spiritual health each day.am I the best in the world? No. the question is: Am I the best I can be?"

Edward James Olmos; Actor & Director.

Continuous growth is the minimum requirement for success. To look at yourself in the mirror and see more than your eyes can see and understand that you have the power to be more than you can see, that is what it means to be alive.

You can always become better than who you were yesterday. It requires a lot of discipline and commitment to personal development to reach the height great men and women reach.

Every day as you step out, whatever you do, ask yourself this question; "am I the best I can be and what can I do to be better?"

DAY 14

"Your life has no meaning until you define it and accept no man's definition of your life, not that of your parents or friends, find your own meaning."

Rudolph Mensah; Author & Speaker

And this definition is not to be done by anyone else but you. Don't allow others to project their definition of life on you. Take a look at yourself and define your own life.

What you want to do, how you want to live and not how society expects you to do or live. It's your life and you have the right to decide. So, decide. You won't decide how you will die and you didn't decide how you were to be born, but you can decide how you live.

Decide today. Define your own life and live accordingly.

DAY 15

"It doesn't matter what is holding you back,
it's never as strong as you holding yourself
back. Most people go through life with their
emergency brakes on, always holding back
and never giving themselves permission to do
anything new. Try and fail but don't fail to
try."

Rudolph Mensah; Author & Speaker.

It is not a matter of who will let you, it is a question of if you
will give yourself the permission to do it?
It is not a matter of "if you can" but "if you will". You have
managed to talk yourself out of anything which challenges you
and have found a way to excuse yourself from doing what you
know you should be doing.
It is never the government, never your parent, never society.
George Bernard Shaw said, "those who succeed look for the
circumstances they need and if they don't find them they
create them." If your environment isn't supportive, create the
kind of environment that will help you thrive. Money can only
hold you back for some time, lack of support will hold you
back for some time, but only you can hold yourself back
forever.

Give yourself the permission to take action on what you know
you should be doing, take your leg off the emergency brake.

DAY 16

"History, though, shows us that the people who end up changing the world- the great political, social, scientific, technological, artistic, even sports revolutionaries- are always nuts, until they're right, and then they're geniuses."

Dr. John Eliot; Author.

When they call you crazy, you are in good company. I am excited when people think I am being nut and what I am thinking of isn't feasible. Yeah, that's how great things come about. Don't expect cheers all the time, expect jeers but keep going. In the end, the world will celebrate you.

Your ideas will not be accepted always and celebrated. If you believe in what you are doing then you don't need everyone on your team to succeed.

Believe in yourself and keep working. Soon, they will applaud you for not giving up.

DAY 17

"Obstacles can't stop you. Problems can't stop you. Most of all, other people can't stop you. Only you can stop you."

J. Gitomer; Author, Speaker & Business Trainer.

Read that again and remember it as you go through the day. No one can stop you but you. Think about it today.

In what areas of your life are you stopping yourself? Think carefully about it and write them down.

Remind yourself to give yourself the permission to do those things you know you should do. Don't stand in your own way.

Look at your life today, what are you stopping yourself from right now?

DAY 18

"Obstacles are those frightful things you see
when you take your eyes off your goals."

Sydney Smith; Writer.

Focus! Commit. Focus on your goals, that way you won't see the storms and the obstacles. There are lots of distractions in the world but if you are concentrated on your goals, you will be saved from a lot of troubles.

In our world today, there are lots of things to take our focus off our goals. It takes self-discipline to ignore the distractions and be focused on what you are going after.

The obstacles are there and as Ryan Holiday explains in his book THE OBSTACLE IS THE WAY, how we see it determines how we deal with it.

DAY 19

"There is no one giant step that does it. It's a lot of little steps."

Peter A. Cohen; CEO of COWEN group.

There is no overnight success. Its takes daily persistent steps to get there. Make sure you don't miss today's step. Keep moving.

Many of us get caught up in being perfect from the beginning, we look at how long it will take for us to get better and get to the top so we don't take the steps at all.

We look at the summit and imagine ourselves there thinking there is a quantum leap that will take us to the top.

It's a process and we must all go through it one step at a time.

DAY 20

"As soon as you truly commit to making something happen, the "how" will reveal itself."

Tony Robbins; Author, entrepreneur, philanthropist and life coach.

Simon Sinek has made "finding your why" popular but as Friedrich Nietzsche first said, "if you know the why for doing something, you can survive anyhow". When you know why you are doing something, then how you will do it is the easiest aspect.

Find your why and the how will take care of itself. Tony Robbins says, finding your why and committing to it is what will lead you to the how which will bring you success.

Have a dream, write down your goals and make the commitment to make it happen. Don't worry about how it is going to happen, all you need to know is why you want to do it.

DAY 21

"Athletes visualize winning 1000s of times before they step on the track. They've already won. Other people just don't know it yet."

Unknown.

Remember, if you can't see it in your mind, you can't hold it in your hands.

You have to see yourself where you want to be even before you get there. I have seen this book, finished in my mind, even before I finished writing and published it.

Your mind should preview what you desire.

Hold on to the image, visualize it and work towards it.

DAY 22

"Every artist was first an amateur."

Ralph Waldo Emerson; Essayist, Lecturer & Philosopher.

Many are afraid to begin. we don't want to be seen as amateurs. I have written crappy articles, I wrote one eBook that was just amateur. My first book has been edited. I am actually going to do a revised edition.

With every new book I write, I get better.

Writing is an art and the more you write and put your work out there the better you become. Many of you think that you just wake up one day and you are a great artist. Begin and practice, every day.

DAY 23

"There is no failure except in no longer trying."

Elbert Hubbard; Writer, Artist & Philosopher.

Don't stop trying. Don't give up, not today, not tomorrow, not the day after. Never, ever stop trying. Change your plans but not the goal.

Today, remind yourself that you will accomplish your goals and it doesn't matter how many failures you encounter on the way, you always have to keep striving for improvement.

We shall win, maybe not immediately but if we don't' quit, we shall definitely win.

DAY 24

"Most of the important things in the world
have been accomplished by people who have
kept on trying when there seemed to be no
hope at all."

Dale Carnegie; Writer & Lecturer.

Yesterday we read that you only fail when you stop trying.

Meditate on this, when you keep trying, you are bound to do
something great which will make you happy and bring
meaning to not only your own life but other people's lives.

When you fail, revise your plan and say to yourself: one more
time. Just one more time, enjoy the process of doing
something great.

When you don't stop, then you shall win.

DAY 25

"Some give up their designs when they have almost reached the goal; while others, on the contrary, obtain a victory by exerting, at the last moment, more vigorous efforts than ever before."

Herodotus; Historian.

It's the fourth month of the year. This is not time to faint and give up on your ambitions. Just keep going after your dreams, victory is only assured when we don't stop.

Persistence is needed in becoming successful, I think it's the universe's way of knowing who really wants it and who just wants it. Those who really want it don't give up easily, those who just want it will give up at the first sight of trouble.

If you give up now, then what were you even fighting for in the first place?

DAY 26

"If you run you stand a chance of losing, but if you don't run you've already lost."

Barack Obama; 44th President of the United States.

You miss a 100% of the shots you don't take. Risk it or lose it, that's your code for today. Never be afraid to stand because you might lose. Barack Obama, who won and lost elections before eventually becoming the 44th President of the United States says "when you don't try, you've already lost."

Today, don't be afraid to try.

I am not afraid of failing, I am afraid of not trying. This has been my life principle. My guiding philosophy. I will rather try and fail than not try and ask, "what if" I tried?

DAY 27

"You can't be that kid standing at the top of the waterslide, overthinking it. You have to go down the chute."

Tina Fey; Actress, Comedian & Writer.

You can't sit at the edge of the pool and keep asking the people in the water "is the water cold"? You have to jump in and find out for yourself.

Many of us are afraid to make that jump of commitment. We really want to swim but we sit at the edge of the pool and contemplate, do I jump or not?

What if I jump and I can't swim; what if the water is cold? Stop asking all these questions; too much analysis leads to paralysis. We are afraid of what will happen if we commit totally to our dreams.

Stop being afraid of what might go wrong and start focusing on what you can do right. Without commitment, there is always hesitancy. Once you commit to it, everything begins to fall into place.

Make the commitment.

DAY 28

"I have learned over the years that when one's mind is made up, this diminishes fear."

Rosa Parks; Activist.

Making a decision is such a powerful thing all other external and internal factors diminish in the face of a made-up mind.

There is nothing as powerful as a made-up mind.

Decide exactly what you want and go out there without fear. Indecision breeds fear and hesitancy, but when your mind is made up, then fear is relegated to the background.

Today, decide, make up your mind and focus on exactly what you want.

DAY 29

"A Quitter never wins – and – a Winner never quits."

Napoleon Hill; Author.

How many times have you heard this? Probably a hundred of times.

I may have heard it a lot more than I can quantify.

Remind yourself today, as long as you are not quitting then you are guaranteed to win. Keep working on your dream.

Quitting doesn't happen in a day, frustration happens over time and as the pressure builds, we finally give up.

Do you remember the guy who gave up? No, no one else does. You will only be remembered if you don't quit. You are already in pain, go on, get a reward for it.

Remind yourself every time, it's not over until you win. If you believe in what you are doing then quitting isn't an option.

DAY 30

"Cultivate your desire for success to be greater than the fear of failure; Failure is merely a pit stop between where you stand and success. Failure allows you to learn the fastest; Failure inspires winners and defeats losers."

Unknown.

Write this in your journal today. Failure inspires winners and defeats losers. It is based on how you handle it.
Failure shouldn't put you down, it should rather inspire you to do more.

Fear of failure has killed many dreams. When you fail, interpret it as a stop on the road which helps you to re-strategize and know what not to do the next time. Don't let failure stop you. If you really want it then let's agree with Henry Ford who said, "failure is only the opportunity to begin again, this time more intelligently".

MAY

It's the fifth month of the year. We are almost through to the middle of the year.

One thing is certain, regardless of how things are shaping up, we have the power and the responsibility to affect the change we need.

Keep the faith alive.

DAY 1

"Winning means being unafraid to lose."

Frank Tarkenton; Football Quarterback.

If you afraid to lose then you don't deserve to win. Think about it.

When we accept the fact that the moment we step out to do anything, we will encounter failure or lose, we don't get overly disappointed when it happens. We embrace the outcome knowing we can give it another shot and we can win.

Learning from our losses is the best way to make the most out of losing when it happens and it will happen.

Being afraid of failing means you will and can never attempt anything great.

You may have the talent to succeed but do you have the gut to fail?

DAY 2

"To be successful you don't need to do extraordinary things, you just need to do ordinary things extraordinarily well."

Jim Rohn; Entrepreneur, Author & Motivational Speaker.

Success is in the little details. Do them well and you will experience the compound effect of success.

Brush your teeth well, lay your bed well, polish your shoes well, write a good to do list for your day, begin the day by accomplishing your most important task. You don't have to worry about the big things, when you build the discipline to be your best even in the little things, you build discipline to do the big things well.

Discipline in any area of life affects your discipline in other areas of life. Success builds up like compound interest. Begin today by resolving to give your best in the little things.

DAY 3

"For every failure, there's an alternative course of action. You just have to find it. When you come to a roadblock, take a detour."

Mary Kay Ash; Businesswoman & founder of Mary Kay Cosmetics.

The only way to find it is to keep looking for it. Don't stop because you failed, keep looking for other ways out.

Life will throw us curve balls, foul them off and keep going. Don't stop. Don't be stopped by failure. If you stop, then you didn't really want to succeed. Life will test you to find out those who really want to succeed and those who just kind of want it.

So, calm down, look around for what you could have done differently and now go out there and try again with the experience you have but don't give up.

DAY 4

"Success is not built on success. It's built on failure. It's built on frustration. Sometimes it's built on catastrophe."

Sumner Redstone; Businessman & Media Magnate.

Embrace every failure. It is bringing you closer to your success. We can learn more from failure than success will ever teach us. Fail fast, fail early and learn your lessons.

There are hundreds of stories of people who came back to succeed massively on the back of countless failures. Don't let it define you, learn from it as quickly as possible and keep moving forward.

Fail quickly, when you fail, learn from it, tuck it under your belt and move on. Everyone who has ever succeed has failed before.

Keep moving.

DAY 5

"First they ignore you. Then they laugh at you. Then they fight you. Then you win."

Mahatma Gandhi; Indian Activist.

Opposition. Negativity. Haters. You can't do away with them once you set out to follow your dreams. Some people sometimes feel like it is their personal business to stop you from reaching your dreams.

When they ignore you, when friends and family don't come close to you anymore because you have set yourself to go on a path they are not willing to join you on, you may be tempted to give up. It's hard and lonely but it's part of the process.

When you don't stop, they laugh at you. They will call you names and they will tell you to stop because you will fail then finally you start showing signs of success. They start fighting you because you are proving yourself right and them wrong. They don't want to lose, they will fight you.

Hold on, you are close to your goal. We shall win, maybe not immediately but definitely.

DAY 6

"I've missed more than 9,000 shots in my career. I've lost almost 300 games. 26 times I've been trusted to take the game winning shot and missed. I've failed over and over and over again in my life. And that is why I succeed."

Michael Jordan (Nike 'Failure' Commercial; 15 Amazing Commercials to Inspire the Greatness in You)

Every failure brings us a step closer to success. If you are afraid to lose you don't deserve to win. The reason why you may not get the results you seek this year is because you are afraid of failing, you are afraid of being embarrassed. You don't want people to laugh at you, you don't want to feel stupid for failing so you wouldn't even try.

Again, I am not afraid of failing, I am afraid of not trying. Don't let fear of failing stop you from trying or going out there to pursue your dreams.

Let's go out today without any form of fear but the confidence to pursue our goals. We shall succeed when we keep going not being afraid of failure or losing.

DAY 7

"In order to succeed you must fail, so that you know what not to do the next time."

Anthony J. D'Angelo; Author & Founder of Collegiate Empowerment

From days 1-6, we have been talking about not being afraid to fail and why failing is even important in succeeding. One incredible thing about failing is that when you learn the lessons, you know what not to do the next time which increases your odds of succeeding dramatically.

Don't run away from failure, maybe the beginning of the year has been met with some disappointments, this is the time to pick yourself up and give it another shot. This time begin again with fresh perspective and renewed faith.
Don't be burned by the same fire twice, you failed? You might as well learn your lessons, you already paid for the tuition.

DAY 8

"I haven't failed. I've found 10,000 ways that
don't work."

Thomas Edison, when inventing the first
commercial light bulb.

I have come to understand that it is our interpretation and
understanding of failure which determines our reaction when
we fail. Someone else once said, "failure inspires winners and
defeat losers".

Either you see it as a stepping stone or a stumbling block.
It all depends on your understanding of what it means to fail.

We grow up with the mentality which confines failure to the
background, when you fail don't even talk about it. It's too
bad, embarrassing, bury your head in shame. You were not
good enough, you can never make it. Failure means you can
never succeed.

Show me how many great men and women you know who
never failed or suffered embarrassment or encountered
adversity in the life? For Edison, failure means I can't get it
done this way, let me move on to the next idea and course of
action.

If plan A fails, there are 25 more letters in the alphabets. Don't
change the goal but you can change the plan or the procedure
but still get it done regardless of how hard it gets. Don't quit,
not today, not the rest of the year and definitely not the rest of
your life.

DAY 9

"As soon as anyone starts telling you to be "realistic," cross that person off your invitation list."

Dr. John Eliot; Author.

Every dream, every idea from the beginning has seemed a little bit ridiculous. Steve Jobs, Bill Gates, Mark Zuckerberg, I can keep mentioning names of those who have revolutionized our world whose idea from the beginning was far from realistic.

When other people don't see what you see and more often than not, not everyone will understand your idea or goal but you don't have to let them discourage you.

John Eliot puts it in a funny way, but seriously if they don't believe in your dreams, why invite them to the celebration of your success?

DAY 10

"We are unlimited beings…we have no ceilings"

Michael Beckwith; Author & New Thought Minister.

We often limit ourselves and what we can do. Harun Yahya once said, "I always wonder why birds stay in the same place when they can fly anywhere on earth. Then I asked myself the same question."

We limit ourselves because we feel comfortable where we are, we are safe, we don't want to encounter the danger of what's out there. The uncertainty is crippling, we would rather stay where we are than go out there even though we are unlimited.

We often have tons of reasons why we are limited but all of that are excuses to me. The ancient men lived in caves, fought off lions and snakes, slept in darkness and ate fruits and hunted wild animals. Did they complain, no, they thrived. Stop complaining and explore the unlimited potential you have inside.

DAY 11

"I've always believed that if you put in the work, the results will come."

Michael Jordan; Retired Professional Basketball Player & Businessman.

Coming from the greatest basketball player of all time (you can disagree but I don't think you will), you may be tempted to think that he got by with talent alone. He was just full of talent but no, he worked harder for what he attained in his professional career.

He did put in the work and he got the results. His standards were high and he competed with himself to bring out the best out of himself.

The results won't come over night, as we step out today, remind yourself to put in 100%. In all you do, increase the effort and stay dedicated, the results will come.

DAY 12

"Some people want it to happen, some wish it would happen, others make it happen."

Michael Jordan; Retired Professional Basketball Player & Businessman.

Stop wishing. Start doing. You have the potential to accomplish all you set out to do today and for the rest of your life.

Don't just desire it, go out there and make it happen. There are three queues in life, which I have extracted from Jordan's quote. The queue with those wanting it to happen, the queue of those wishing it will happen and the queue of those making it happen.

Which queue are you in?

The queue wanting it to happen, the queue wishing it will happen or the queue making it happen?

DAY 13

"I didn't get there by wishing for it or hoping
for it, but by working for it."

Estée Lauder; Manufacturer & Marketer of
prestige skin care products

In order to take action, to move from just wishing to doing, you have to understand what needs to done in order to act. If you dream of starting your own consultancy business, pause, think about the things that will help you to get started. Do not just fantasize about how wonderful it will be to own your consultancy business. Stop dreaming about how life can be enjoyable when you finally build your business.

Develop a plan of action, get to work on what you are dream about.

DAY 14

"Only those who dare to fail greatly can ever achieve greatly."

Robert Francis Kennedy; Former United States Senator.

The greater the risk, the higher the reward. That as simple it can be explained. If you are afraid of failing then you can't possibly achieve anything worthwhile.

This is not about taking "stupid" risk in order to fail greatly but taking intelligent risk, protecting the downside and not being afraid to take action because of failure.

Failing defeats losers but inspires winners.

Is there anything worthwhile which is never going to be difficult or without the risk of failure?

DAY 15

"But it ain't about how hard you hit. It's about
how hard you can get hit and keep moving
forward. How much you can take and keep
moving forward. That's how winning is done!"

Sylvester Stallone; in the movie "Rocky".

When I finally got to watch this movie, it was the year 2016.
Life can be pretty tough and only those willing to go through
the quagmire can get to the beautiful island.

You are sure going to take some hits, you are really going to
face oppositions and challenges but your tenacity and
persistence will determine whether you will succeed or fail.

So, again, today, no matter how hard you get hit, take it in
your strides and keep going. That's how you win.

DAY 16

"Our greatest glory is not in never falling but
in rising every time we fall."

Confucius; Philosopher.

We are all bound to fail, at something. Unless of course you don't try anything, which means you have failed by default as J. K. Rowling describes it.

I believe that life is about getting back up every time you get shoved down, and you will get shoved down.

As kids, learning to walk, how were we able to it? We got back up again and again after every fall and that's how we learned to walk.

We all fall down in life but only the successful get back up and that's what's glorious in life.

Falling down is allowed but getting up is mandatory. Don't stay down, the ground is no place for a champion.

DAY 17

"Defeat is not the worst of failures. Not to have tried is the true failure."

George Woodberry; Literary Critic & Poet.

Do I believe this? Yes, 100% with all of my soul, my body and spirit. Life is about creating memories and not regrets.

I don't want to grow old and talk about what could have happened if I had tried or given it a shot.

I want to talk about what happened when I tried. Most people stay in their corner afraid to come out because they are afraid to try their idea. Afraid to pursue their dream because they don't want to fail. They don't want to be ridiculed or embarrassed.

But hey, no one is getting out of here alive. So, you can either die in the game or on the sidelines. I want to die in the game, with my head in the game. Try everything and never stop living.

Go out today with the confidence that you can try all your ideas and get in the game. You have been a spectator for far too long.

DAY 18

"The difference between successful people
and others is how long they spend time feeling
sorry for themselves."

Barbara Corcoran; **Businesswoman, Author,
Speaker & Investor**

We all fail at something, if you haven't you will. If you don't it means you didn't try anything new. You merely lived your life following laid down conventions and following the norm.

If only you are trying out your ideas, working on your dream, you are going to encounter failure. Now, how you deal with it will determine whether you will succeed or not.

I have written books which didn't sell. I have in fact not made any real money from my first books. They have only set the ground for me as an author. Now, do I feel sorry for myself or do I go on to write my fifth book?

Yeah, this is my fifth book and I have the sixth in line to follow in a few months.
Dust yourself after every defeat, learn your lessons and go out there and keep working. There is no point in brooding on who did what and who hurt you and what someone said about you. Suck it up, that's life.
Deal with it and keep moving.

DAY 19

"The size of your success is measured by the strength of your desire; the size of your dream; and how you handle disappointment along the way."

Robert Kiyosaki; Businessman & Author

The "strength of your desire", how bad do you want to succeed? Do you just kind of want to win or you really want to? Are you just wishing or are you willing to roll up your sleeves and get to work?

The "size of your dream", small dreams don't inspire you. Big dreams pull you and take you all the way. A dream which isn't big enough doesn't scare you and doesn't make you want to get better. If your goal is to do something you know you can do, what difference will that make? Your dream should be big enough to make you grow into the person who can accomplish that dream. The new you.

Finally, the disappointments will come. "How you handle them", how much courage to begin again will determine whether you will succeed or fail.
Think about this today, is your desire strong enough, your dream big enough and are you well equipped to overcome disappointments?

DAY 20

"It is hard to fail, but it is worse never to have tried to succeed."

Theodore Roosevelt; 26TH U.S. President & Hero of the Spanish-American War.

Failure is hard. Yes. I have failed before. Again, and again. For some of them, I was well prepared, I had done everything right but still failed.
It's hard. It's heartbreaking. I can't begin to tell you how people look at you. The embarrassment, the shame, the pain. Its unbearable, but none of that can be compared to the pain of regrets.

I had a man in my consulting room who had lots of regrets. He told me about a special school he wanted to build 30 years ago but never did. Fast forward, he is 79 now and not only is he not having the money, he also doesn't have the energy. Even after I tried to encourage him to take it up and get a team of young people to work with him, he was just full of regrets.

I couldn't look into his eyes. It was teary. So, he could have failed if he tried to start the school. But that cannot be compared to the pain in his eyes because he never tried.

I don't fear failing, I fear never trying.

DAY 21

"Failure is not falling down, but refusing to
get back up."

Deamsian Wisdom;

In a boxing match, you don't lose when you fall down, you lose when you don't get up again. Falling down is allowed and getting up is mandatory if you want to win.

You may have come crashing down with some of the projects you started this year. Don't stay down. Get back up.

Try again. Fail, try again. You ask, for how long?
Until and unless you succeed. Let your desire be stronger than failure.

Don't stay down.

DAY 22

"That some achieve great success is proof to all that others can achieve it as well."

Abraham Lincoln; 16th U.S President

This has always been my motivation. If other people can do it, I can also do it. It doesn't give me my own pattern of becoming successful but the fact that others in my community have been able to become successful in their life, it is a clear indication that I can also have my name among the greats.

If you are looking for a sign today, look around you and write down the names of the people in your community or nation who have done exploits. If they did it, you can do it. Some of them were in a much more difficult situation than you are but still succeeded.

Avoid the excuses, it's not rocket science and even if it is, you can learn.

DAY 23

"I am always doing things I can't do. That is
how I get to do them."

Pablo Picasso; Prolific Artist

You say you haven't done it because you can't do it.

But have you tried? Have you ever tried?

Most of us hide behind the idea that we can't do something
when we haven't even gone out to try it.

Other people say it can't be done when you haven't done it
yourself, you join them in echoing the fact that it can't be
done.

Let Picasso inspire your today, do the things you think you
can't do then you will begin to do the things you think you
can't do.
Today, there is nothing you can't do. Believe it.

DAY 24

"A diamond is a piece of charcoal that handled stress exceptionally well."

Unknown.

In the world today, everyone is stressed up. Unless of course you are not pursuing any goal.

Challenges are inevitable in life and our ability to withstand the challenges life throws at us determines how strong we stand in order to succeed.

We have to endure the storm to get to the other side. A diamond is expensive because of the process it goes through to become a diamond. It either stays a charcoal or goes through extreme processes to become a diamond.

It's okay to be a charcoal or any carbon element but in order to become a diamond you must be willing to endure the pressure and the stress.

Today, ask yourself, do I want to remain a charcoal or become a diamond?

DAY 25

"It is our experiences that mold us into who
we are…. during times of adversity our true
character will show."

Unknown.

As we read yesterday, our ability to endure the challenges we
face in life give us the experience we need which in turn makes
us who we are.
So, today, whatever life throws at you, go through it. Endure
it. Don't quit, don't complain, you can go through it and you
will get to the other side and encourage others to do same.

King Solomon of ancient Israel said in the book of Proverbs
that "if you give up in the day of adversity, your strength is
small." Strong people don't buckle down under pressure, we
may fall but we always find a way back up.

Be resolute in your mind, I will survive every test, for without
the test, there will be no testimony.

DAY 26

"The greatest mistake you can make in life is to continually be afraid you will make one."

Elbert Hubbard; Writer, Publisher & Artist.

If you never made a mistake, you never tried anything new, Einstein once said. As long you are trying, you will make mistakes. Wear them like a battle badge, learn from it, be proud that you tried and get better.

If you live in perpetual fear of making a mistake, that is the biggest mistake you will ever make. Many choose to be spectator instead of getting in the game because they are afraid of making a mistake.

Let me tell you something, you are going to make mistakes whether you are in the stands or in the game. Don't die without fighting for your dreams because you were afraid of making mistakes.

DAY 27

"Seventy percent of success in life is showing up."

Woody Allen; Filmmaker, Writer & Actor

How true is that? So true. You just have to show up and opportunities will start opening up, doors will be opened for you.
Don't sit home today complaining about how everyone is shutting you down, no one is helping you and nothing seems to work for you.

Imagine you are looking to meet a pretty girl and perhaps fall in love. If you sit in your room, chances are you will meet no one.
When you go out there, chances are you may still meet no one but again, you have 50% chance of meeting someone when you go out there.

So, your best option is to just go out there. You are looking for a job, if you don't send application letters no one will call you. If you send letters, still you may not get any calls but you have a 50% chance of someone calling you for a job.
Woody Allen, highly optimistic gives it a 70% chance of succeeding. I am with him. So, today, it doesn't matter how you feel, just show up.

DAY 28

"The only time you run out of chances is when
you stop taking them."

Unknown.

When do we stop trying? Never, until we succeed. Life will always come our way with opportunities. We only sometimes do not recognize it because either we are looking in the wrong places or not paying attention.

So, be ready and prepared to take every chance coming your way today.

You are never out of chances, you will be offered chances, the sad part will be when you are not ready to take up the chance you are offered.

DAY 29

"I have stood on a mountain of no's for one yes."

Barbara Smith; Restaurateur, Model & Author.

Optimism keeps you going even in the face of adversity. The world is not going to hand what you seek to you on a silver platter.

Don't expect people to do things for you because you want it. The way will be stony and there will be a lot of people telling you no.

I interpret every NO as Next Opportunity. I don't fear rejection or embarrassment. I am simply moving on to the next.

If you know what you want, the no's you get on the way shouldn't stop you from believing there is a yes along the way.

Perhaps, throughout the year, things haven't gone the way you expected. You have had a lot of no's, keep going, there is a yes coming.

DAY 30

"Sometimes good things fall apart so better things can fall together."

Marilyn Monroe; Actress, Model & Singer

How is the year going? Are things falling apart? Are you facing difficulties and challenges which seems to overcome you?

Maybe your relationship just ended, you lost someone important or something important.

Some people believe that everything happens for a reason, I believe that we can find a reason for everything that happens.

If things are falling apart, don't fall with them. Go through it and stand strong.

Believe that things will come together for you. Don't fall with them.

DAY 31

"Action is the foundational key to all success."

Pablo Picasso; Prolific Artist.

I wrote about this in my book LEAP: ACTION; THE BRIDGE BETWEEN KNOWING AND DOING which is available on Amazon.

We can dream all we want, meditate all we want, imagine all we want, until we get up and take action on our dreams, they remain mere wishes.

Taking action however small will make the biggest difference in your life.

Today, decide to act on your dream. Do something, however small. Too much analysis leads to paralysis.

You have thought about it for far too long, it's time to take action.

JUNE

It's the sixth month of the year.

Let's take some time to be grateful for the gift of life and for the family and friends we share our lives with. This is month of gratitude.

DAY 1

---

*"Every day do something that will inch you
closer to a better tomorrow."*

Doug Firebaugh, Sales and Marketing Coach

This has been my guiding principle in life. Don't get too
caught up in fretting about when you will make it or get there,
just commit to getting the best out of today.

A lot of us also spend most of our time brooding over the past
and the mistakes we made. We can never change yesterday but
if only we can commit to making the best of today, we are
making a good down payment for tomorrow.

Let this be your principle, too. Put in your best today for a
better tomorrow. I would recommend John Maxwell's book
TODAY MATTERS to you. It will surely help you make the
best of everyday you live.

DAY 2

"It is not enough to stare up the steps, we
must step up the stairs."

Vaclav Havel; Former President of the Czech
Republic.

Action. Yeah, not talking, not wishing, not dreaming, not
imagining, not meditating, not affirmations but action.

This is something perhaps the law of attraction doesn't teach
you. Most people think they can just wish for things to
happen, after you are done thinking and dreaming, you have to
actually take action.
Beginning is always the hardest but that's the only way to get
something done, by doing.

Today, stop staring, start climbing your stairs. You have stared
at it for far too long, make the step.

DAY 3

"The secret of life isn't what happens to you,
but what you do with what happens to you."

Norman Vincent Peale; Minister & Author.

Things happen to us, lots of them out of our control.
Someone may cut you off in traffic today, that's out of your
control, what's in your control is how you react.

That's the secret of life as Norman Vincent Peale opines.

As you step out today, remind yourself that even for the things
which are out of your control, how you react to them is in
your absolute control. Bite your tongue before you reply that
person making sarcastic comments about you. Breathe in and
out before you make a comment. It hurts but you can always
walk away with your integrity and dignity intact.
Again, we go through different phases of our lives, not all of
them are good experiences but the most important thing is
what you do and how you get the positives out of what
happened. Don't let what you go through define you, let it
refine you.

DAY 4

"We all have ability. The difference is how we use it."

Stevie Wonder; Musician.

Everyone is talented. Few are disciplined. That makes the difference.
Each and every one of us here on earth has the ability to do something he or she is best suited to do. Everyone has the ability to accomplish something great.

Why do some excel in their chosen fields and others just drift along?
It is the daily discipline and how we commit ourselves to develop our abilities that determines those who succeed and those who don't.

Today, are you willing to put in the work or are you just going to sit on your potential denying the world of your abilities?

DAY 5

"Many receive advice, only the wise profit
from it."

Harper Lee; Novelist.

Wise people take advice. If you find yourself loathing advice and rejecting corrections, you are a fool. There are lots of advice on the internet, sift through them. There are lots of books out there with solutions to your problem.

Buy the book, read it from cover to cover and find the solution to your problem. When you get advice, ask yourself what can I do with this?

Apply what you learn and get better. Don't just listen and brush it off. Listen to grown-ups, you don't have to follow everything they say but listen and profit from it.

"Reprove not a scorner, lest he hate thee: rebuke a wise man, and he will love thee. Give instruction to a wise man, and he will love thee. Give instruction to a wise man and he will be yet wiser: teach a just man, and he will increase in learning" (Proverbs 9:8-9).

Wise people are always looking for feedback, looking to find out what they did wrong, and what they could have done better. Wisdom is opened to correction.

Be opened to feedback; both positive and negative.

DAY 6

"If you don't go after what you want, you'll never have it. If you don't ask, the answer is always no. If you don't step forward, you're always in the same place."

Nora Roberts; Author.

I remember a friend of mine first wrote me this quote after high school. I had been writing poems and I always wanted to publish my poems in a daily newspaper called the "Junior Graphic" in Ghana.
I kept writing the poems and never took any action on sending the any of my poems for publication.

And she wrote me this quote! It changed me.

Many of us are in the same place because we assume we can never get what we want, that the answer will always be no when we never even asked. Always afraid to fall when we have never even taken a step forward.
Let this quote ring in your mind today, always go after what you want. Ask and risk being told no, but ask anyway. Step forward, take the first step and don't stay in the same place.

You will never know what will happen until you try.

DAY 7

"If you do what you've always done, you'll get what you've always gotten."

Tony Robbins; Author, entrepreneur, philanthropist and life coach.

I love Albert Einstein's quote, "insanity is doing the same thing over and over again and expecting a different result."

If you want to make a change in your life, you have to change something you do every day. As I thought about it, I wanted to experiment with something trivial I do every day.

So, I put myself to the test and started to brush my teeth with my left hand instead of my right as I always do. After three attempts, I unconsciously went back to using my right hand. So, I asked myself, what other things have I been doing unconsciously that I haven't even taken notice of?

That is how we build habits and our habits determine who we become.
Are you looking for a change, change something you do every day. Develop new habits. Do something different from the way you have always done it.

DAY 8

"Don't get bogged down with all the details of how it's going to come together. Just do the dishes. And watch the momentum build."

Brian J White; Actor.

We get so worried about the outcome when all we can control is the process.

Enjoy the process, do something small today, tomorrow and the next and watch the results compound. We focus so much on the destination we forget about the process. If you are not enjoying the process, you are less likely to enjoy the destination.

Don't worry so much about how or when you are going to finish or get there, focus on a step at a time and just keep going.

Today, don't stress it, focus on making the best use of today and watch the rest unfold.

DAY 9

"The best preparation for tomorrow is to do today's work extremely well!"

H. Jackson Brown Jr.; Author.

We can't predict tomorrow neither can we control it but we can prepare for it.

One again, I will quote Whitney Young, "it's better to be prepared and not have an opportunity than to have an opportunity and not be prepared."

Commit fully to making the best of today and you don't have to worry about what comes up tomorrow. Why? You will be ready for tomorrow.

We often wonder about how tomorrow is going to be, how our future is going to be when what we should be focused on is how we can make the best of today. Over the last few days, we have talked about the importance of focusing on today and making the best out of it.

Preparation is key in becoming what you dream of, how are you going to prepare today?
People are rewarded in public for what they do private. It takes lots of hours of hard work and preparation before getting to the limelight.

How are you preparing today for your tomorrow?

DAY 10

"The secret of getting ahead is getting started."

Mark Twain; Writer, Humourist & Lecturer.

Just start. Stop talking. We are in the middle of the year and perhaps you are still talking about what you want to do this year.
We are halfway through, when are you going to start?

Start today and now. The earlier the better. Don't look too far down the road and worry about how far you have to go, take inspiration from how far you have come and just begin.

No more delays, start today. Close the book right now and get to work.

DAY 11

"The person who never made a mistake never
tried anything new."

Albert Einstein; Theoretical Physicist & Nobel
Prize Winner

Mistakes are proof that you are trying.
It is not a mistake to make a mistake but it is a mistake to
repeat a mistake. You have to learn from it and do it better the
next time.

Don't run away from making mistakes unless of course you
are not willing to grow. New ideas, new thoughts, nothing
comes out already formed, you have to be willing to work on
them and make mistakes therefore learning from them.

Mistakes are for our learning not repeating but never be afraid
of making mistakes. I looked at this book over and over again,
wondering if I should publish it?
Have I made mistakes, have I actually made a mistake writing
such a book? Who even needs it? Is it good enough to go out
there?
I was never going to know the value of this book until I had
enough courage to publish it and see the how it does.
Could I have done better, of course, I see all my books to be
so. Couldn't I have added some things, yes, there is always a
new perspective but the only thing I can guarantee is that, if I
should do something like this again, it is going to be a 2.0
version of this one.

DAY 12

"The best way to predict your future is to create it."

Abraham Lincoln; 16th U.S. President

How do you that?

It is dependent on your DAILY DECISIONS. The things we do every day compound into what we become. At the very moment you are on Instagram browsing through pictures, browsing through snapchat flowers, liking pictures on Facebook, ask yourself if what I am doing is helping me create a better future or taking me away from the future I desire?

What we do today, the tiny decisions we make today will compound into how our future will shape up tomorrow.

So, if you are wishing to be slim and fit in the future, then look at what you are eating today. If you want to be smart and intelligent in the future, what are you reading today?

You see, this is not magic, everything we are doing will have an impact ten, twenty years to come.

Before you do anything today, ask yourself, how will this impact my life twenty years to come?

DAY 13

"Even if you're on the right track, you'll get
run over if you just sit there."

Will Rogers; Actor.

Maybe the year is going very well for you and you are just about getting complacent. I placed this quote here to remind you that the only way to get better is to keep going. You are good but keep working to get better and when you get better, don't stop until you become the best.

Progress is what we should strive for. Every day, we should be focused on progressing in our chosen field of endeavours.

Never sit for too long or park for too long, you will get run over.

DAY 14

"If you have time to whine and complain
about something then you have the time to do
something about it."

Anthony J. D'Angelo; Author & Founder of
Collegiate Empowerment

Today, make a promise to yourself; no complaining, no
whining, no cursing, no getting angry over the amount of
sugar in your cup of coffee.

Be solution oriented, never focus on the problem.
Stop talking about problems, stop whining and stop
complaining.

Train yourself to always look out for solving problems and
you shall be rewarded for it. It is easy for anyone to complain
but it takes matured people to find solutions.

If a pipe leaks in the house, your five-year old daughter can tell
you that the pipe is leaking. She can't fix it. What will you do
then?

You find a solution.

DAY 15

"Don't live life in the past lane."

Samantha Ettus; Author & Speaker.

We all make mistakes but the best thing is to stop stoking the fire. You don't have to continue being foolish. You made a mistake the first time doesn't mean you have the license to keep on making them. It doesn't also mean you should moan over what happened forever.

Feeling sorry for yourself won't solve the problem. I know, your daddy wasn't there, your mum abandoned you, you were abused, yeah, what are you going to do about it now?

You came out of it, you have your scars to show. Now, go into the future with all your energy. What's ahead is better than what happened in the past. We all have our stories, we don't go about telling everyone who cares to listen.

Don't get burned by the same fire twice. When we don't learn from our mistakes, what is the point? And if you have learned, what's the point in brooding over the past? **Why do you keep looking back when you are not going that way? Focus on where you are going.**

DAY 16

"The thing that is really hard, and really amazing, is giving up on being perfect and beginning the work of becoming yourself."

Anna Quindlen; Author, Journalist & Columnist.

We are often held back with the idea of perfection. We are attached to the popular adage, practice makes perfect.

No, I am sorry but practice doesn't make perfect, practice brings improvement and you can always improve on any level you are. If you think you are perfect then you are done growing.
Growth is one thing which makes humans capable of achieving the impossible. No matter how good you think you are, you can always get better. You can always begin to work on becoming better than you are now.

When you focus on becoming your best, you have to do away with the notion of being perfect. Most people want to be perfect and are afraid of allowing themselves to leave the familiar to becoming better.

Be yourself, work on yourself and become your best. Forget about being perfect.

DAY 17

"He who fails to plan, plans to fail."

Unknown

This is one of the quotes I read as far back as grade 6. I still cherish it. Planning is an essential aspect of becoming successful.

If you have no plan, how will you even know what you accomplished?

No one makes a plan to become overweight, no one makes a plan to fail his or her exams, no one makes a plan to lose money, no one makes a plan to be forty and broke, these things happen when we don't make plans.

What plans have you made for today, this week and the rest of the year?

What's your plan for the next ten and twenty years of your life?

If you are failing to plan then you are planning to fail.

DAY 18

"Imagination is the beginning of creation.
You imagine what you desire, you will what
you imagine and at last you create what you
will."

John C. Maxwell; Author, Speaker & Pastor.

This process as described by Maxwell is the process with which how many inventions have been made, breakthroughs in technology in our world.

Our mind is a powerful weapon and if only we can learn to harness the power of our imagination, we will be living a limitless life.

Imagine what you desire, will it, and then comes the most important aspect, create it.

We can only accomplish it by taking action (creating it). Most people just imagine and affirm what they desire but never get to the last part of creating it.

After your imagination, get to work, create what's in your mind through action.

DAY 19

"And the day came when the risk to remain
tight in a bud was more painful than the risk it
took to blossom."

Anaïs Nin; Essayist & Novelist.

Many are held back by the fear of losing and never venture into anything with the slightest risk. Afraid of making mistakes, afraid of being embarrassed, afraid of losing.

Someone once said, **"if you don't take risk, you can't grow, if you don't grow, you can't succeed, and if you don't succeed you can't be happy and if you can't be happy what else are you living for?"**

So, in order to be happy in life, there is the need to take risk and risk-taking means taking action. Yeah. Act on your ideas, act on your dreams before they fade away.

Don't worry about when you will get it done, just start. I love small beginnings. Winning always takes care of itself when you are ready to start small while thinking big. Don't be so caught up with figuring everything out before you start, just begin and things will start falling into place

Let today be the day when you decide you are not going to remain in the bud. It's time to blossom.

DAY 20

"The major difference between the big shot
and the little shot is the big shot is just a little
shot who kept on shooting."

Zig Ziglar; Author, Salesman and Motivational
Speaker.

You only fail when you stop trying you remember?

Yeah, many are looking to hit the jackpot quickly but there is
nothing like that. The people you admire, the great men and
women you are so in love with, only become great with
consistent practice and improvement of their craft.

Persistence and consistency are the keys to excellence. Be
persistent and you will get it, be consistent and you will keep
it. You are looking for your big break, don't stop trying for
you never know which opportunity is coming your way.

Today, don't stop shooting, keep shooting and the next shot
might be your big shot.

DAY 21

---

*"When you come to the end of your rope, tie a
knot and hang on."*

Franklin D. Roosevelt; 32nd U.S. President.

When you live life always expecting something positive to
happen, something positive is going to happen.

There is no denying the fact that the unexpected happens in
life, we lose people we love, we lose jobs and relationships we
expect to last forever end abruptly.

When life takes a dip, what do we do?

Just hang on. Trust that a way out will come. When we begin
to feel positive and look out for opportunities, doors which
seemed closed all of a sudden begin to open.

Stop panicking, tie a knot and hold on, plan and the solution
will come to you. Stop struggling, be calm and begin to look
out for the positives.

Does it seem like you have come to the end of your life? Tie a
rope and hang on.

DAY 22

"Feel the fear and do it anyway."

Susan Jeffers; Psychologist & Author.

Are some people never afraid? Everyone becomes afraid at a point in life, almost every time a decision has to be made. Fear will come up in our face all the time but in order to succeed, let's take Susan's advice, we should feel the fear and do it anyway.

Don't let the fear hold you down and keep you from going after your dream. We have discussed extensively in this book the need to blast through our fear with faith. Fear will always show its ugly head in our lives and we need to defeat it every time before we can move forward.

Everything you want is on the other side of your fear. When we go through the barrier of fear, we grow into the kind of person who is well prepared to succeed.

DAY 23

"Nothing in the world can take the place of persistence. Talent will not; nothing is more common than unsuccessful men with talent. Genius will not; unrewarded genius is almost a proverb. Education will not; the world is full of educated derelicts. Persistence and determination are omnipotent. The slogan 'press on' has solved and always will solve the problems of the human race."

Calvin Coolidge; 30th U.S. President.

A man who as a President didn't make huge historical decisions left the world with a huge historical statement. He may not have sent America to the moon or fought wars but as good as a leader can be, this quote to me is one above everyone else.

Persistence will surely overcome every adversity. You only fail when you stop. With this quote in mind, no obstacle is too big. I just have to keep working at my plan.

I read this to myself anytime I encounter challenges. Persistence will wear down every barrier to our success. Never stop swinging, don't stop trying and don't simply stop.

Because if you don't stop, if you persist you shall succeed.

We shall win, maybe not immediately but definitely if we persist.

DAY 24

"Don't say you don't have enough time. You have exactly the same number of hours per day that were given to Helen Keller, Pasteur, Michelangelo, Mother Teresa, Leonardo da Vinci, Thomas Jefferson and Albert Einstein."

Life's Little Instruction Book, compiled by **H. Jackson Brown, Jr.**

The average person thinks in term of time as morning or afternoon. The above average thinks in term of hours. The successful person thinks of half hours while the very successful person thinks in term of minutes.

Studies reveal, 60-80% of people don't even know how they spend their time.

Chances are, most people fall into the average group. We go to work in the "morning" not "8:00 AM". We send emails in the afternoon not "1:30pm". Until we begin to think of time as hours and minutes and allocate how much time we spend on each task, we are likely to achieve little.

The beggar has 24 hours and the billionaire has 24 hours. How do you think of time?

DAY 25

---

*"When I believe in something, I'm like a dog
with a bone."*

Melissa McCarthy; Actress, Comedian &
Writer.

We have all seen a dog with a bone, right?
Yeah, you can't take it away from it. When we believe in
something, we should make a firm commitment to it to hold
on.

So, the best person to believe in is yourself. When you believe
in yourself, never let go of the conviction that you shall
succeed. People will try and talk you out of your dreams,
circumstances will knock you off guard but just like a dog with
a bone, never let go off your belief.

I believed this book will be different and it will change your
daily routine. I was like a dog with a bone when people told
me there are lots of quote books out there, I simply said, "this
is not another quote book" and it isn't.
Hold on to what you believe, the world will try and knock you
off.

DAY 26

"Worrying is the same thing as banging your head against the wall. It only feels good when you stop."

John Powers; Author & Motivational Speaker.

There is a difference between thinking and worrying. Most people even when they are worrying mistake it for thinking.

When you worry, you only rehearse what went wrong or could go wrong, you magnify your fears and postulate what may never even happen.
When you think, you are looking for solutions. You are looking for a remedy.

When you realize that you are no longer thinking but worrying, stop. Use your mind to think not to worry. Jesus Christ gave a compelling reason in the Bible why worrying is useless.

"Has anyone by fussing in front of the mirror ever gotten taller by so much as an inch?" – Jesus Christ, Matthew 6: 27 The Message Bible

DAY 27

---

*"We need to start work with the idea that
we're going to learn every day. I learn, even at
my position, every single day."*

Chanda Kochhar; CEO of ICICI Bank.

A Chinese proverb says, "He who knows not and knows not that he knows not is a fool." We must be willing to learn from everyone because they have something to teach us. I have learned a lot just by observing and listening to others. I have had great friends and mentors who have shaped me. The only way to learn is when you are ready. So, there is a saying that, when you are willing to learn, nothing can stop you and when you are unwilling, no one can teach you.

Wherever a seminar is going on, if the theme is of interest to you, go and learn. Go to church, be willing to learn. Ask questions. Wisdom is always excited to fill up people who are thirsty for her. You will find it when you are ready and desirous of wisdom.

If you don't show the desire to learn, no one will teach you anything. So, develop that insatiable desire to learn. No one will take time to teach you when you feel you know it all. Never make the mistake of thinking that you know it all. No man is a reservoir of wisdom. That is why we are admonished to learn, relearn, unlearn and learn again.

DAY 28

"You can't give up! If you give up, you're like everybody else."

Chris Evert; Tennis Player.

You remember the guy who gave up? Yeah, no one else does. No one said it will be easy, if they did, they lied to you.

It's not easy but it worth it. There is a verse in the book of Proverbs of the Bible which says, "if you faint (give up) in the day of adversity, it means your strength is small."

Strong people don't go down easily and even when they do, they always get back up.

Don't be like most people, most people give up.

DAY 29

"Discontent is the first necessity of progress."

Thomas A. Edison; Inventor & Businessman

If you like where you are why would you fight to get to someplace different?
You have to decide that you don't like your current state, you don't like the results you are getting or you are not satisfied with the life you are living before you can make progress. Only then can we begin to think of what to do in order to make progress.

What would you like to change? Write it down. Don't worry about what you are discontented about, think about how you can change it.

I told you one of my goals this year is to learn how to write movie scripts, that is because I have always had issues with some of the movies I have seen.
Therefore, I have decided to write the kind of movies I want to see. The only reason why I am learning to write script because I am discontented with some of what I see.

What are you discontented about?

DAY 30

"No one can hurt you without your consent."

Eleanor Roosevelt; Politician, Diplomat, Activist & Former First Lady of the U.S.

Call me names, I won't respond. Tag me with labels, it won't stick, I am simply aware of myself I don't care what you think of me. Neither your praise nor your criticisms affect me.

These days we break down because of what someone said about us on Facebook. We have become a soft generation. We are depressed because we didn't get enough likes on Instagram. We care so much about what other people think of us we don't even know what we think about ourselves.

Stop worrying about who likes you, do you like you?

How you react to hate will determine whether you will be hurt or not.
Don't even give it attention. What you give attention you promote. This has been my guiding principle in life, I hope you adopt it as well.

JULY

We begin the last half of the year. We still have enough time to turn around and get things done.

This is the month of new beginning. Regardless of how the first half of the year has gone, we can always start afresh.

Let's keep working.

DAY 1

"Change your life today. Don't gamble on the future, act now, without delay."

Simone de Beauvoir; Writer & Philosopher.

Gambling is counting on luck or chance for something to happen. You have no control over the outcome when you gamble.

So, in order to be happy in life, there is the need to take risk and risk-taking means taking action. Yeah. Act on your ideas, act on your dreams before they fade away.

I love small beginnings. Winning always takes care of itself when you are ready to start small while thinking big. Don't be so caught up with figuring everything out before you start, just begin and things will start falling into place. You can't always see the end and even more true, you don't have to see the end. This is not about winning or losing. Often, it is who you become when you begin that is important and not what you get. What you get is only a reward for who you become.

DAY 2

"This journey has always been about reaching your own other shore no matter what it is, and that dream continues."

Diana Nyad; Author.

For people who are looking at something bigger, it is not about winning and everyone else losing. It is about something more than getting to a finish line because there is no finish line. There are only achievements on the road which we stop to celebrate momentarily and then we are on to something else.

Continuous process of growth and realization of self requires action and that is what makes life worthwhile. How do we do that? We have to take a leap and grow our wings down.

We all have the other side of our shore to get to, we must strive for the rest of our lives to get to this other part of our shore regardless of the opposition we encounter.

It's your journey, complete it.

DAY 3

"When I'm tired, I rest. I say, 'I can't be a superwoman today.'"

Jada Pinkett Smith; Actress & Businesswoman.

Rest is an essential part of the journey to our dream. We will get tired, we will feel fatigued. Don't beat yourself up when you can't wake up at 4:00 am one day.

Be comfortable with pulling on the sheet and getting an hour more of sleep. Don't get burned out trying to prove you are a super person all the time.

Rest affords us he time to rebuild and replenish our lost energy.

Be comfortable with it. When you need to rest, do. This is not about making it a habit to rest anytime you are tired. Winners know it is important to stay in the best kind of shape to be able to take the opportunities when they come.

Rest when your work is done. Before you begin the next project make sure you have had enough rest to begin the next one. Rest is essential and it is often a reward for those who work hard.

After God created heaven and earth and everything that is in it, HE rested.

DAY 4

"Don't look at your feet to see if you are doing
it right. Just dance."

Anne Lamott; Novelist.

Just keep doing it, every day. This has been my principle.
Don't be afraid to put it your work out there. Don't try to be
perfect, just do it, get better.
As you get better and strive for progress, you will one day
wake up and realize that people see your work to be perfect.

Stop judging every move you make. Stop trying to please those
who are looking, enjoy what you are doing as much those who
are watching. Just dance.

The only to do that is to concentrate on doing it and not so
much about how you are doing it. Winning takes care of itself
when we concentrate our efforts on doing it.
Today, as you step out there, just work, just write, just paint
and remember that as long as you are doing it, every stroke is
making you better and better.

DAY 5

"I hear and I forget. I see and I remember. I
do and I understand."

Confucius; Philosopher.

Practice they say makes perfect, it doesn't, it brings
improvements. Deliberate consistent practice is important to
becoming better at what you do.

Don't just listen to motivational messages, sermons and be all
pumped up about changing your life only to slump back to
your old life.

What you have to do is to wake up and practice it, do it, when
you do, it etches into your mind. Action is the one thing which
separates the successful from the unsuccessful.

What are going to do today?

DAY 6

"Beyond getting inspired after reading a self-help post, the more important question is – what do you intend to do now with that information?"

Article: Are You a Self-Help Junkie?

Yesterday we talked about practicing what we hear or see. What are you going to do after you have read today's quote or even as you are reading this whole book?

It is not only about reading and sitting down. Do something with it.

You have come across lots of quotes from the beginning of this book. The question is, when you put this book down or when you close this book on your device, what are you doing to change your own life? Don't be satisfied with stories, how other people are doing it. Go out and do it for yourself too.

DAY 7

"The challenge is not to be perfect...it's to be whole."

Jane Fonda; Actress & Writer.

The fear of not being perfect. The fear of not being enough. The fear of not being tall enough, short enough.

Sometimes in life we believe we are not enough, what we have is not enough. This concern of our inadequacy stops us from pursuing our goals.

We are not good enough, not pretty enough, not handsome enough, not tall enough, not old enough, not fat enough, not fluent enough, not fair enough, not rich enough.

You see, just as we focus on our inadequacies, we also have our strengths. Let's turn our attention to those things. I am not tall enough but my height is just great for me, I am not fair enough but my dark skin is a gem, I am not good enough in speaking French, I can speak English languages fluently, why dwell on your insufficiencies when you can focus on your strength.

You are enough and the only thing wrong with you is you buying into the idea that you are not enough.

DAY 8

"The final mystery is oneself."

Oscar Wilde; Poet & Playwright.

Don't we all go out there to look for meaning? Secrets to riches and principles for success?
We go chasing after 30 ways to succeed, 71 ideas to become a millionaire. 13 ways to be happy.

17 ways to have a lasting marriage. I have read a lot of them. I am not saying they don't have meaning but listen, the final mystery is yourself.

If you understand yourself enough, then you will know what you are good at, your weaknesses. How you relate to others, how you react to situations will all change if you really get to know yourself.
You wouldn't need steps and ideas, you will know how to make everything work in tune with your personality.

Do you know yourself?

DAY 9

"If you just set out to be liked, you would be prepared to compromise on anything at any time, and you would achieve nothing."

Margaret Thatcher; Former British Prime Minister.

Your ideals won't be accepted by all. Not everyone will like you, I have said it before, this was the truth which took me a long time to grasp.

The truth is, if you are looking to please people then you can't live by your principles and your beliefs. You will compromise and the world is full of people who have compromised on their beliefs, their dreams and have chosen to stand in line when they were created to stand out.

You have to go against the tide to make a difference. You have to be willing to be hated sometimes and to be ignored. In the end, if you stand by your ideals the world will stand with you but never try to compromise on them because you don't want to offend anyone.

You won't achieve anything by becoming like everyone else.

DAY 10

"When you embrace your difference, your DNA, your look or heritage or religion or your unusual name, that's when you start to shine."

Bethenny Frankel; Television Personality & Entrepreneur.

Come to terms with who you are. Accept yourself and your past. Don't be ashamed of where you come from, don't be ashamed of the name you carry, don't be ashamed of the mistakes you have made.

Be yourself and let the world accept you for who you are instead of trying to become who you are not.

You are you and that's the truth. Embrace your imperfections and be confident enough to live your life only then will you begin to shine.

DAY 11

"All that we are is the result of what we have thought."

Buddha; Spiritual Teacher

My favorite book says "as a man thinks in his heart so is he." It is an established fact that our thoughts control our habit and our habit determines what we do. This becomes our character and whether we succeed or not, it goes back to the fundamental truth about our thinking which is our thought.

As you step out today, remember that your mind will only reproduce what you feed it. Feed your mind with positivity and you will have a positive life.

"Summing it all up, friends, I'd say you'll do your best by filling your minds and meditating on things true, noble, reputable, authentic, compelling, gracious – the best, not the worst; the beautiful, not the ugly; things to praise, not things to curse." – Philippians 4:8 MSG

DAY 12

"If you can't go straight ahead, you go around
the corner."

Cher; Singer & Actress.

Life is not a straight line. It never is. It may seem so when we
are starting out. We may have been made to believe to go to
school, get good grades, get out of school and get a job. Get
some good money, get married, raise wonderful kids and retire
at a good age.

Special announcement: it's not that simple. I grew up with this
roadmap in my mind. I thought my dad will grow up with me
but he died. I didn't know I would fail a course in school but I
did. I have encountered failures.

Did I stop? No, I went around the corner. I turned my scars
into a story. I am writing about them to encourage others, I
am speaking to others about it. Don't worry if the path doesn't
lead you straight ahead. We have a saying in Ghana which
goes: there are many ways of killing a cat.

Same here, there are many ways of becoming successful. There
are many ways of fulfilling our dreams. When we can't go
straight ahead, join me, let's take the corner. I don't mean
cheating, I mean being resourceful in finding alternative ways
of getting things done even when it seems there is no way out.

DAY 13

"Watch your thoughts; they become words.
Watch your words; they become actions.
Watch your actions; they become habits.
Watch your habits; they become character.
Watch your character; it becomes your
destiny."

Lao-Tzu; Philosopher.

This sequence doesn't need my commentary. This is true and has been throughout the ages. It's all begins in our minds, what we think, we become.

The Bible, one of the oldest books in the world, says, "as a man thinks, so is he". Years after that, Napoleon Hill wrote his famous book THINK AND GROW RICH.

Our mindset determines our conversations and they become what we do every day. So, if you don't like what you are seeing in your life, go back to what you are thinking, go back to the basic software of your brain.

Alter your mindset and alter your life.

DAY 14

"Whether you think you can or think you can't
– you are right."

Henry Ford; Captain of Industry & Business
Magnate.

Yesterday, we read about our mindset and how it affects our
habits and our destiny.
What we think determines the outcome of situations we face
in life according to Henry Ford.

You can choose to be afraid or you can choose to have faith.
You can choose to think it won't happen or you can choose to
think it will happen but know that whatever you think the
outcome will be will likely be.

Choose to be positive. Believe you can and you will.

DAY 15

"A pessimist sees the difficulty in every opportunity; an optimist sees the opportunity in every difficulty."

Winston Churchill; Former British Prime Minister.

We are all aware life is full of challenges, being optimistic doesn't mean you decide to turn a blind eye to the difficulties of life. It is about believing that the outcome will be positive regardless of the current difficult circumstances.
What do you get by remaining negative? Stay positive.

This book can fail, this book can succeed. It's difficult to write this book. The work involved, the research, but also this is an opportunity to do something I have always wanted to do as an Amazon author. But why do I have to concentrate on the challenges and not the opportunities? I use this to simply illustrate to you the need to be looking at the brighter side. It doesn't mean you run away from reality, be fully aware of the situation but choose to believe something positive is coming out of it.

When you encounter a difficult situation, choose to see the opportunity in overcoming it. Think in terms of solutions and not of challenges.

DAY 16

"I do not try to dance better than anyone else.
I only try to dance better than myself."

Arianna Huffington; Author &
Businesswoman.

It's you versus you, make sure you win. That's all I have for you today. It is not about the person next door, it's not about becoming better than someone, it is about your own progress.

Just as you concentrate on becoming your best, you may end up the best. Always, remember, it's you versus yourself. As you go out today, make sure you win.

Progress they say equals happiness. Progress in your own potential, be better than the person you were yesterday.

DAY 17

"There is more hunger for love and
appreciation in this world than for bread."

Mother Teresa; Roman catholic nun &
Missionary.

There are millions out there who feel disrespected, not valued, not appreciated. They live under the starvation for appreciation and love. As you step out today, be sure to spread some sunshine, show love.

We don't have to do it for only those we know, the person you meet on the street could do with your smile. Stop to ask how she is doing. She may be dealing with a lot and would be glad to have someone show she cares. I know, you have your own storms but the beauty of life is when we are able to hold onto our own pain and help others.

This brings us a lot of fulfilment at the end of the day. If you can go to bed at night feeling you made even one person's life easier because of something you did, sweetheart, you had a good day. God will be happy with you.

DAY 18

"A man can do all things if he will."

Leon Battista Alberti (1404–72); Author, Artist,
Architect, Philosopher & Priest.

It's all begins with a dream and a plan then the will to do it. It is not a question of if you can, it is a matter of if you will?

When a man decides he will do something, the universe conspires to bring all the forces together to set you on the path to making it possible.

It's about the decision to begin. If only you will, then you can.

Are you willing to do it? Don't worry about how you are going to do it. Don't stress about how you can raise the capital to get it done.

The question again is, are you willing?
Where there is a will, there is always a way.

DAY 19

"You have to 'Be' before you can 'Do' and 'Do' before you can 'Have'."

Zig Ziglar; Author, Salesman and Motivational Speaker.

When we seek success, we often look at "having" or "becoming" but that's only the end product.
To begin, you need to first "become" the kind of person who merits what you want to "have."

You first have to "be" a hardworking, disciplined and committed person. You have to become who you were not before you can "do" what you weren't doing. Take action, do something every day in the direction of your dream then you can have what you want.

You realize that who you become by having what you want is more important than what you get in the end. You become a different kind of person. a person who is disciplined and committed and can get things done.

DAY 20

"It's impossible until it's done"

Nelson Mandela; Former President of South Africa.

There may be no evidence of your dreams coming true but no one ever knew Barack Obama could become the president of America. None believed before April 1954 that someone could run a mile in less than 4 minutes. No one ever imagined we could go to space. You should know there are many things that have happened in the world which were initially perceived to be impossible. There have been scientific theories that have been disproved but were held sacred for a long time.

There was a time when we never thought we could have cars, airplanes, trains, ships; all the machines that we have now. Technology has virtually set the world in a constant speed. You literally have to run to stand still. It has amazed us all. We are moving at a fast pace such that you stop for a second and you may be left behind. Technological advancement in medicine has improved our healthcare and solved diseases we thought years ago were without cure or untreatable. There was a time when we never thought airplanes were possible; we had experts on hand who said if God wanted us to fly He would have given us wings.

"Flight by machines heavier than air is unpractical (sic) and insignificant, if not utterly impossible."-Simon Newcomb

There were scientific theories to back this belief and for a long time many people believed in it until the Wright brothers set out to write history and flew 18 later months at Kitty hawk after Simon made that statement. They had to overcome the fear of failure and the fear of what people will say: "these boys are crazy; how can they think of making something that will fly? That is impossible!".

They didn't listen to the naysayers, the worrywarts. They committed to working on the idea and they overcame the fear of failing and made it possible.

Consider the radio, mobile phones, printers, medical equipment, the television, the electric bulb, the computer, space travel, internet and every other technology you have around you — these are all things that were once thought impossible. Generations in the past never believed there will be a time that these things will be common place in our time. Now they are so common we don't even stop to think about them. I believe if people from the 50's, 60's and 70's appear in our time they would think we are aliens or some creatures from another world, with all these technologies which surround us. Even people from the 80's marvel because of how fast technology is taking over our lives.

In the past, trains were thought impossible. It was believed by experts with all their might that if a human being travels in anything more than 15 miles per hour he is likely to go mad or even suffer from asphyxia, today there are automobile trains travelling 200 miles per hour and we are not going mad or dying from asphyxia. If ever the words of these men were paid any attention, we wouldn't be here:

"Rail travel at high speed is not possible because passengers, unable to breathe, would die of asphyxia," Dr. Dionysius Lardner (1859) concluded with a clear conviction.

And Martin Van Buren (1830) added by a note to the President: "Dear Mr. President: The canal system of this country is being threatened by a new form of transportation known as 'railroads' …As you may well know, Mr. President, 'railroad' carriages are pulled at the enormous speed of 15 miles per hour by 'engines' which, in addition to endangering life and limb of passengers, roar and snort their way through the countryside, setting fire to crops, scaring the livestock and frightening women and children. The almighty certainly never intended that people should travel at such breakneck speed."

One person, Sir William Preece, Chief Engineer of the British Post Office in 1878 had condemned the idea of telephones, "The Americans have need of the telephone, but we do not. We have plenty of messenger boys".

It was impossible for two people to talk through a wire many miles apart. No one ever dared to believe there will be some time human beings could talk miles apart through a wire. These days we don't even need wires to talk, we have "wireless" communication devices.

We have also gone past just talking on the phone over long distances apart but we now send pictures, videos, documents and even money on our phones.

The computer was also deemed impossible. To own a computer even after its invention was a luxury and only the privileged few could own one. The military and the banks were among the privileged few who were using computers. It needed a large space and couldn't be moved around.

We see happening today, things that were perceived impossible. Like what Ken Olson (1977) said, that, "There is no reason anyone would want a computer in their home," or that, "We will never make a 32-bit operating system," as said by Bill Gates.

Today computers are part of us and more sophisticated and smarter. Today's computers do almost everything for us. The computer is a virtual extension of our lives.

Now, if only you will commit to your dream, you can make everything possible. Also, pause and reflect on this idea: **If generations were convinced that all these things were impossible but they are now common things we use every day then there are things you see as impossible which are only impossible in your mind.**

There are dreams you have that may seem impossible only because of limited knowledge and ignorance. If you could only look beyond the negative vibes in what people say, what you have read in the papers and get to work, you will make the impossible possible.

The word impossible does not exist in today's dictionary for me. It shouldn't be used because everything is possible, either now or tomorrow. Where there is limited knowledge and/or ignorance, the word impossible exists. Generations ahead of us will do things we deem impossible today.

Be informed however that cars did not just appear, television did not just appear, the airplane didn't fall from the sky, smartphones didn't just pop up, what was impossible only became possible through the faith, hard work, dedication, commitment, consistency, persistence, patience and sacrifice of people who believed they were possible. People made the commitment and overcame their fear. They took the plunge and moved in the direction of their dreams.

Whatever we see in our lives as impossible we can turn them into possibilities if we get to work on them.

DAY 21

"Instead of thinking outside the box, get rid of the box."

Deepak Chopra; Author & Public Speaker.

Yesterday I gave a lengthy dissertation to Nelson Mandela's quote because I love it so much. Today, I will leave you to meditate on this and write down your own thoughts. You can share them with me.

We think in the boundaries of what we know, our beliefs, religion, geographical location but the world is too big to be having a myopic view of events.

Get rid of your narrow perspective, your prejudices and be open to possibilities.

DAY 22

"Normal is not something to aspire to, it's something to get away from."

Jodie Foster; Actress & Producer.

We are not here to conform to the norm. I am not here to fit in and conform to the normal. I am here to disrupt the status quo. Follow my own path and leave a trail for others to follow.

Many of us are raised in a society which wires into our brain to choose safety. Get a safe job, make sure you don't disrupt the system, don't chase chances. Don't try, you will fail.

When you fail they will laugh at you, you will be embarrassed. That's the normal but if you are looking to make a difference in people's life, get away from normal.

Be different.

DAY 23

"You see things and you say 'Why?' But I dream of things that never were and I say 'Why not?'"

George Bernard Shaw; Playwright & Political Activist.

Everything we see around us were other peoples' imaginations and they asked the same question: why not?

Steve Jobs asked, why not a smartphone, why not a personal computer?

Bill Gates asked, why not personal computer software?

The inventors of the past and our time have all asked this same question, Edison asked, why not an electric bulb?

Allow your mind to imagine and then resolve to make it happen. Everything is possible as we read a few days ago.

So, what have you been thinking about and ask yourself, why not?

DAY 24

"Stop thinking in terms of limitations and start
thinking in terms of possibilities"

Terry Josephson; Businessman.

We all have them, we have our limitations, we have our
inadequacies but they shouldn't stop us.

We should be focused on what's possible, we should be
thinking in terms of solutions not the challenge. When we use
our imagination, we begin to see the possibilities.

If we can change our mindset, we will begin to see the
solutions
which surprisingly lie around us but we are blinded from
seeing them because we are focused on the limitations.

DAY 25

"When you feel copied, remember that people can only go where you have already been, they have no idea where you are going next."

Liz Lange; Fashion Designer & Entrepreneur.

Do I ever get worried someone copied me or stole my work?

That was my yesterday's work, I am working on something better today and you don't even know about it.

The only people who get mad about people copying them are those who are at a standstill. If you are progressing, someone copying you shouldn't be a problem.

Keep moving, he or she will always be behind you. You are always step ahead of the game. By the time someone copies this idea, I am on to the next. You can't run away from being copied. I may have copied other people when I was starting out.

Don't waste your time fighting off those who are copying you. Keep moving. Get better. Keep creating.

DAY 26

"If you want things to be different, perhaps the answer is to become different yourself."

Norman Vincent Peale; Minister & Author.

You attract what you desire based on the person you become. It takes a lot of discipline and commitment to change yourself.

It's easy to talk about what you want, dream about it but it takes discipline to change yourself, to become that person who can become what you dream of.

Habit is such a powerful thing, most of the things we do in life are habits. This means we do them without thinking.

It takes a lot of energy to say, today, I won't watch tv, I am going to read. It takes a lot of discipline to say, I am not going to watch movies on Netflix, I am going to work on my writing or painting.

If you want to see a difference or make a difference in the world, you have to become a different person. You can become different by developing new habits.

DAY 27

"If the grass is greener on the other side,
maybe that's because you're not taking good
care of your grass."

Unknown

The comparison paradigm is one you may never get out of if you don't concentrate on your own life. Often, we are forced to see other people's life as perfect especially in a social media era.

We see photos on Facebook, we see pictures on Instagram, we begin to think others have it all together and our lives are in a mess.

Keep your head down, work on your grass and believe that you shall get what you seek if you invest your time and energy instead of looking at what others have.

We are all in the process, keep your head down and work. Work on your grass and you will be too busy to notice if someone's grass is greener or not.

DAY 28

"If opportunity doesn't knock, build a door."

Milton Berle; Comedian & Actor.

We don't wait for opportunities to come to us, we move, we work and along the path they come.
I have had the opportunity to do a lot of things because I started doing something first.

Mostly those things didn't seem important but in the end, they were the doors I was building.
I blogged for a year before my book came out. I built a following on social media and got myself readers who were always reading my articles.

I was building my door. You are dreaming of writing your own book,
start by writing for the local newspaper, write for your school's magazine. Get your work out there, someone might notice your work and give you an opportunity. Stop complaining about what you don't have and do something with what you have.

DAY 29

"If you're not making some notable mistakes along the way, you're certainly not taking enough business and career chances."

Sallie Krawcheck; Author.

Mistakes are proof that you are trying. Don't be saddened by it, neither feel bad or broken by your mistakes. It only means you are not afraid to try your ideas.

The more ideas you try, the more chances you take, the probability to making a big break. Don't tiptoe through life trying not to make mistakes.

Dare yourself, do it, learn from it, do it again. You are only getting better. I have made mistakes; big ones and I am still making them only that I am getting wiser with every mistake.

Don't be held back, go and try your idea, go make mistakes and learn fast.

DAY 30

"The question isn't who is going to let me; it's
who is going to stop me."

Ayn Rand; Novelist.

No one can stop you but you. The world paves way for the
one who knows where he is going. Obstacles may stop you
temporarily, challenges may stop you for a moment but if you
decide to quit, then that's the end of the game.

So, always give yourself the permission to pursue your goals,
don't let the temporal defeats and challenges stop you because
no one is actually going to stop you if you are determined and
committed.

If you are not stopping yourself then no one can stop you
from getting to your dream.

DAY 31

"If you light a lamp for someone else, it will also brighten your path."

Buddha; Spiritual Teacher

Today is the last day of the month, we are still on the journey to our dreams. Often, we think more of ourselves. Today, decide to do something nice for someone, a stranger possibly and see how much joy that brings you.

Helping other people brings me such joy that I can't describe with words on this page.

Giving books away, helping others, doing free speaking events for hundreds and I always come out much happier. I received a letter from a young boy who sat in class while I spoke in one school, the content of the letter brought me unspeakable joy.

Go out today and light a lamp for others and your own path will be brightened.

AUGUST

It's the eighth-month of the year.

We have an obligation to continue pursuing our goals. Take some time to review your goals for the year. How are you doing on them?

Set your goals for the month and remember that if it is going to happen it depends on you.

DAY 1

"Thousands of candles can be lighted from a single candle, and the life of the candle will not be shortened."

Buddha; Spiritual Teacher

We begin this month with another one from Buddha.

Think about this: we should spend our life making other people's life better and so when we live this earth, they can say of us, here goes a man or woman whose life gave meaning to many.

We ended the month of July with a quote from Buddha admonishing us to light others candle for them as it brightens our own path. This is a continuation of the advice. Helping other people won't make you any less of a human being.

As you go through the day, ask yourself "how many candles are you lighting up in the world?"

DAY 2

"If your actions inspire others to dream more, learn more, do more and become more, you are a leader."

John Quincy Adams; 6th U.S. President.

What kind of life are you living? Are you affecting others or you are living only for yourself?

The definition of leadership isn't in your title or the name on your door. It is not a matter of the number of degrees after your name, it is as Quincy simplifies, inspiring people to dream more, learn more and become more.
You don't need an office, you don't need a title, you need a heart and the ability to make a difference in other people's lives.

However small it may be, if you can always make one person dream more, learn more and become more, you're a leader.

If you can do that for yourself, you are leading yourself down a successful path.

DAY 3

"The true measure of a man is how he treats someone who can do him absolutely no good."

Ann Landers (Esther Pauline); Columnist.

How do you treat the janitor and the CEO?
You bow before the CEO and lord it over the janitor?

If you are the CEO, how do you treat the investors and the security man? Do you kiss the feet of the investor and fail to smile at the security man on your way in?

Life has a funny way of putting us in positions making us feel invincible sometimes but no one is. In life, make sure to treat people who are below you with respect and love.

Treating each other with respect is an epitome of maturity. That's the essence of humanity.

DAY 4

"All blame is a waste of time. No matter how much fault you find with another, and regardless of how much you blame him, it will not change you"

Wayne Dyer; Philosopher, Author & Motivational Speaker.

Don't we all love to make excuses?

Blaming others gives us temporal relief as it takes the responsibility away from us. If I can blame someone else for my inability to finish the project or get something done then I don't have to live with the consequences.

But do we really think blaming others and finding faults ever did anyone good?

Own your stuff. You failed, own it. You slipped, own it. Take responsibility for it. Put the blame on yourself.

The moment we make the decision to own our mistakes and take responsibility for our lives, we begin a new path to self-discovery and self-mastery.

I blame no one, everything happens because of me and I have the power to change it.

DAY 5

"If I stop to kick every barking dog I am not going to get where I'm going."

Jackie Joyner-Kersee; Athlete.

If you know where you are going, don't let the distractions distract you. People will sneer at you, jeer at you, call you names but don't let it distract you.

Focus on where you are going, you don't have to stop and reply to every hate comment about you. You don't have to explain yourself to cynics who are hell bent on frustrating you. Just keep going in the direction of your dreams. Don't let small minds disturb you.

The really great people make you feel great, the small-minded people try to put you down. People who don't feel good about themselves also don't want you to feel good about yourself.

Those who don't like you probably don't like themselves. Forget them and keep your head up towards your dream.

DAY 6

"You are the one that possesses the keys to
your being. You carry the passport to your
own happiness."

Diane von Furstenberg; Fashion Designer.

Everything is on you. How many times have we been told
this?
We often seek without what is within. Happiness is something
you make for yourself. No one owns your happiness.

When we base our self-worth and happiness on external
factors we lease control and power to things we have no
control over.

There is no key to happiness, the door is always open.
Understand that you are in charge of your life and you are the
master of your soul.

Be in charge. Be happy.

DAY 7

"Great minds discuss ideas. Average minds discuss events. Small minds discuss people.

Eleanor Roosevelt; Politician, Diplomat, Activist & Former First Lady of the U.S.

Which category do you fall into? I have often used this as my test to access whether I am being great, average or small.

If I find myself talking about people for some time, I knock myself out of it. I tell myself, Rudolph, you are behaving like a small-minded person.

If I catch myself discussing a lot of football games and entertainment shows with friends, that's me being average.

I tune myself therefore to talk about ideas. It's not always easy talk about ideas when others merely want to talk about last night's game.

Go out today and be a great person. Talk about ideas.

DAY 8

"Knowing what must be done does away with fear."

Rosa Parks; Activist.

Clarity. Yes, knowing exactly what to do get rid of the fear. When there is uncertainty about what to do, there is always bound to be fear of what might happen.

It is therefore important to develop a clear goal for every project you embark on. You may not see all the way down but you need to know what exactly you are about to do.

This way, you can do away with the fear which comes with lack of clarity on what you want to do. Do you know exactly what you want to do?

DAY 9

"You cannot push anyone up the ladder unless
he is willing to climb."

Andrew Carnegie; Industrialist.

Don't waste time pushing people up who don't want to be
pushed. It is the will to do it which is a major determining
factor in who climbs the ladder and those who don't.

This applies to us. If you are not willing to do something, it
doesn't matter how much inspired we get or what's in it for us,
we won't do it.

I wanted to do this, so I did it. There were other things I could
have done, friends presented opportunities to me but I politely
said no.
It is always the will to do something which bridges a dream to
reality.

DAY 10

"Hate is like acid. It can damage the vessel in which it is stored & destroy the object on which it is poured."

Ann Landers (Esther Pauline); Columnist.

The damage to the vessel it is stored in is often damaging. Why hate?
It's too much of a burden. The interesting thing is that, often the person you are hating isn't even aware you are hating him or her.

The person is having a good time. Forgiveness is a powerful tool to free ourselves from hate. It's not about who is right and who is wrong, forgiveness frees us of pain and diseases from hating.

Don't destroy yourself, let it go. Forgive and forget. It's healing to your soul and body.

DAY 11

"You are the average of the five people you
spend most time with."

Jim Rohn; Entrepreneur, Author &
Motivational Speaker.

"He that walketh with wise men shall be wise: but a companion of fools shall be destroyed." – Proverbs 13:20 KJV

It seems quite obvious, right? Not really! A lot of people don't get this simple concept.

Someone once said, "Your association determines your destination." Another wise man opined, "If you fly with pigeons, you will end up becoming one." Another one goes: "If you lie down with dogs, you are going to get up with fleas." Jim Rohn also said succinctly, "You are the average of the five people you hang around the most."

One more: "If you hang around nine broke people, chances are you are going to be the tenth broke person." A lot of things are contagious; so is wisdom and foolishness. Cold and hot water cannot co-exist in a bucket. One thing will happen for sure: Either the cold water turns the hot water cold or the hot water turns the cold water hot. Almost always, the cold water turns the hot water cold.

If you go for a walk with someone, one of two things will happen: either you adjust to the speed of your friend or he adjusts to yours. In the end, you will both not walk with different speeds; you will unconsciously slow down if you are walking faster or speed up if you are walking slowly.

The point is, the people you associate with determine how far you get in life. You can't hang around people who slow you down. Sometimes it's okay to leave some people behind. Not everyone will get into the future with you. Be careful, therefore, of your association. They say, "Show me your friend and I will show you your character." Amos 3:3 says, "Can two walk together, except they be agreed?"

Who are your friends? You can't choose your siblings but you can choose your friends. Have an introspection and leave out some people who keep dragging you down. I am attracted to wisdom and so I listen to tapes, read books, talk to and learn from friends who are full of wisdom

Walk with the wise and become wise; if you are already wise, become wiser. It is said that if you are the wisest one in your group, you have to get a new group. Surround yourself with smart people and be challenged to get better every day.

DAY 12

"I attribute my success to this: I never gave or took any excuse."

Florence Nightingale; Statistician & Founder of Modern Nursing.

Excuses get nothing done. We are often tempted to give or take excuses. It always sounds good.

Benjamin Franklin once said, "anyone who is good at giving excuses is seldom good at any other thing".

There are two things in life, we are either making excuses or getting results. Those who are fond of making excuses never get anything done.

You are looking to succeed? Take excuses off the table. However, the year has gone so far is probably because you have been making a lot of excuses.

DAY 13

"You can waste your lives drawing lines. Or
you can live your life crossing them."

Shonda Rhimes; Screenwriter & Producer.

Life has no limitations. Every limitation we see is self-imposed. It's true sometimes we have barriers in our lives but truly, if we want to go over, we will.

We often stop ourselves, draw lines and make some places no go areas. We restrict our own growth and lose our sense of adventure.

Life is too short to spend it wondering what if? So, go over the lines, take some risk. Try your ideas, go over the limitations and you will see how much fun and fulfilling life is.

Being in the medical profession, I had a line to cross into writing books and speaking. I could have drawn a line about what I will do and not do. I am glad I crossed that line.

Go out today and see beyond the lines society has set for you, the line you have set for yourself. Still, it's a choice and like Shonda says, you can choose to draw them or cross them.

DAY 14

---

*"I'd rather regret the things I've done than
regret the things I haven't done."*

Lucille Ball; Actress, Comedian and Model.

What is regret? Looking back and agonizing on something you should have and could have done. We can also regret something we did but shouldn't have Many people live with regrets.

Life should be lived forward. When we always live in the past and brood over what could have and should have, we are wasting our time.

That's regret. There is no use brooding over what you could have done. Make up your mind to not miss the next opportunity. Decide to act on your ideas.

Do them now, forget about what's in the past.

There is no use for regretting what you didn't do.

DAY 15

"So, you have some enemies…good, that
means you stood up for something!"

Winston Churchill; Former British Prime
Minister.

Obviously, the moment you take a stand in this world, there
are people who will make it their personal business to hate
you.

Remember not everyone is like us and will be like us. Every
belief has an opposing belief. Every stand you take has an
opposite stand. As Newton said, every action has an equal and
opposite reaction.

So, when you stand up for good, expect a reaction. This is to
say when you stand up for something you believe in, expect
opposition. This doesn't necessary mean every opposition is a
supposed enemy. Sometimes they are people who out of love
wouldn't let you make mistakes. Discern who is out for your
best interest and who is out to stop you.

Bottom line, don't be disturbed when people oppose you.
People only oppose you when you stand up for something.
When you conform, no one cares. They ride with you.

DAY 16

"Always bear in mind that your own resolution
to succeed is more important than any other
one thing."

Abraham Lincoln; 16th U.S. President

Do we even have to care what people think of us? It is our own self-belief and confidence in ourselves which sets the tone for our success.

There is nothing as powerful as a made-up mind. If you decide that you will then you can.

The year might have been going in the wrong direction. You might have incurred some losses, had some failures but be resolute about ending the year at your best and begin today working towards it.

Your own resolution is the number one determining factor in you becoming successful.

DAY 17

"Always make a total effort, even when the odds are against you."

Arnold Palmer; Professional Golfer.

The fact that you made the resolution to succeed doesn't mean everything will fall into place. The odds may be against you but never lower your efforts.
Give 100%. When you are tired and all you want is to quit, don't.

When we started, I knew I had to work twice as hard to get half of what they have. I knew I didn't have enough. I wasn't endowed with enough material things. Not enough books, not enough money, not enough wealthy family members, not enough support, not enough encouragement, didn't attend a first-class school, grew up in a village I still call home but I was supposed to run the race with others who had more than enough.
What do you do when you come to the playing field and you are not endowed as others?
You would expect that they would make room for your inadequacies. You will be given a bonus point to compensate for what you don't have. You will be favoured because you don't have shoes. You will be made to start ahead because of your weakness.

The sad thing is that, the rules don't change for you because you come into the race with a disadvantage, you are not treated differently, you are expected to run the same race for the ultimate price---win the gold. Nobody has time to listen to you cry about the spilled milk. No one has time to hear you talk about your disadvantages once we all sit at the table. The moment you take a seat at the table, you are expected to play regardless of which cards you were dealt with.

You don't have any aces, kings or queens in the cards you were dealt with, you still have to play to your strength.

You may be injured during the game because you have no shoes. You may slip during the race but none of that will count in the end.

The game doesn't stop for you to heal just because you bruised your arm. There is no time out for you to get back on your feet, you have to learn to do that yourself quickly. No one will wait for you just because you got tired. Life keeps on moving and you must. Your inadequacies are excuses and excuses are not needed in the arena of champions.

So, how do you then run this race when you have already lost from the perspective of the game? According to the laws of nature, according to the rules of the game, from the standpoint of the people, you can't win without shoes, without enough money, with no connections, when you don't have enough, you can't win!

Always believe you can win, don't let what you don't have stop you from doing what you can. Believe in yourself and believe in what you are doing.

DAY 18

---

*"Numbing the pain for a while will only make
it worse when you finally feel it."*

Albus Dumbledore, "Harry Potter" character

Yesterday, we talked about fighting from a position of
perceived weakness. When you come up against great odds,
you are likely to suffer some pain. Don't mask it, don't
pretend, don't run away from it, face it. Feel it, cry if you want
but don't quit, scream if you want but you are not allowed to
quit.

Don't anaesthetize yourself against the pain.

Many of us pretend we are not hurt, we pretend to be happy
when deep inside us we are tearing apart. It's alright to cry.
You don't appear weak, you appear brave.

We can allow our tears but not our fears. So, when you feel
the pain, when it hits you hard, allow yourself to go through it.
Recover successful and go out there in the morning as if you
were not crying last night.

DAY 19

"Difficulties should act as a tonic. They
should spur as to greater exertion"

B. C. Forbes; Journalist & Author.

Great people rarely have an easy past. Everyone who ever
made it to the top has endured some level of adversity. It
didn't discourage them, it was rather their motivation. What
kept them going forward even in the face of overwhelming
challenges.

Life would be boring if we never encountered any difficulties.
When we do encounter difficulties, let us not give up or give
in, let them be stepping stones instead of stumbling blocks.

Endure. You shall come out better.

DAY 20

"Do not bring people in your life who weigh you down. And trust your instincts ... good relationships feel good. They feel right. They don't hurt. They're not painful. That's not just with somebody you want to marry, but it's with the friends that you choose. It's with the people you surround yourselves with."

Michelle Obama; Former First Lady of the U.S.

Your association determines your destination, right? Who is your friend? Who is in your inner circle?
Choose them. Don't let them choose you. When people choose you, make sure you choose them too. Have friends who compliment you, help your personal development and rob off on you. Iron sharpens iron.

You walk around with five foolish people chances are you will be number six.

Are you becoming a better person or not but the relationships you are in? take some time to evaluate your relationship and ask where it is leading you.

DAY 21

"Valour grows by daring, fear by holding
back."

Publilius Syrus; Writer.

After High school, I developed the interest in writing. In
college, I was runner up for best Student writer. I wrote
articles, stories, I never knew when I would become an author.

I thought I wasn't good enough. Not skilled enough. Maybe I
was right. How else was I going to become a writer if I was
afraid of putting my work out there?

So, I wrote one book. Then another. Then another. Then
another. With every book I put out there, I grew in
confidence, the belief that I can do it become profound.
In my first year as a rookie author, I put four books out there.
Some people advised me to take it easy. I began this year, not
knowing how many books I really wanted to write but I
started.

By the end of the month of January, I had ideas for four
books apart from this one which I thought about last year.
My fear has been relegated to the background and my
confidence is growing.
Will you dare or will you hold back on your dream?

DAY 22

"What we hope to do with ease, we must first learn to do with diligence."

Samuel Johnson; Essayist & Writer.

Every master you see has failed a lot more times than the beginner can ever imagine. It doesn't happen overnight.

You don't wake up one day a successful writer. You don't wake up one day and win the Olympics 100m race. It takes hours and hours of preparation.

Hard work and commitment, consistency and persistence to get to the point where you don't sweat it anymore.

You have to be willing to do the things others won't do today so you can do what others can't do tomorrow.

Diligence means doing it with discipline, whether tired or not, whether you feel like doing it or not.

Whatever your dream is, you must first decide to do it diligently till it becomes a habit.

Diligence yields dividend.

DAY 23

"You can never leave footprints that last if you are always walking on tiptoe."

Leymah Gbowee; Peace Activist.

What are you afraid of? You don't want to offend anyone. You don't want to make mistakes. You don't want to be embarrassed.

You don't want to be ridiculed.

You can't live your whole life not wanting to upset the status quo. If you don't climb, you won't fall but what joy is there if you spend your whole life on the ground?

Dare to be different. Go out there today and be determined to leave your mark at your work place, with your friends, in school, in church.

Let the world know you were here, that your presence made a difference and not just a statistic.

DAY 24

"Four steps to achievement: plan purposefully, prepare prayerfully, proceed positively, pursue persistently."

William A. Ward; Writer & Baptist Missionary.

Plan purposefully: It begins with a plan. This is the road map you create for yourself and the path you travel. It has to be definite and clear as much as possible.

Prepare prayerfully: I believe in prayer and the potency of it. When you make your plans, pray over it. Commit it to God.

Proceed positively: you will surely be faced with several obstacles which may force you to quit but go in addition to believing you can accomplish it, take positive action on it.

Pursue persistently: Persistence. The word which makes everything possible. If you are persistent, you will get it.

DAY 25

"In the middle of difficulty lies opportunity."

Albert Einstein; Theoretical Physicist, Nobel Prize Winner.

Wrapped inside every problem is the solution.

With every problem or challenge comes with it a potential reward if only we commit to finding the solution. Wherever there is a problem, there is a solution. If there is no solution, then it's not a challenge.

We don't have to run away from the challenge.
We need to face it and find the solution in there.

Opportunities we seek are wrapped up in the challenges we run away from. Anything which irks you is probably something you should work on solving because in the middle of it is the opportunity to do something great.

DAY 26

"You don't need applause and cheers all the time to succeed, there may be jeers, it should spur you on, eagles don't need pigeons clapping for them to fly, keep your head down, fly higher."

Rudolph Mensah; Author & Speaker

Most people spend their whole lives looking for support. Someone has to stand by them before they can do something. We need support groups, we need people hailing us, we need people singing our praise before we can do anything.

Alone, we can do nothing. We are always looking to see who is with us before we begin.

No, the successful people in life don't need crutches all the time. They don't need someone to say good things about them to make them feel good.

When someone says something bad about you, you feel bad, when someone says something good about you, you feel good, have you given your remote control to someone?

If you are looking to fly like an eagle, if you are looking to do great things, remember that you may have to do a lot of things alone. You may not get the support, you may not get the praise but if you know and believe what you are doing, don't let that bring you down. Fly on your own!

DAY 27

"Winners embrace hard work. They love the discipline of it, the trade-off they're making to win. Losers, on the other hand, see it as punishment. And that's the difference."

Lou Holtz; Former American Football Player.

In becoming your dream, hard work can never be taken out of the equation. Work is a principle God instituted right from the beginning.

God blesses your hard work. You can't be blessed when you are lazy. God doesn't bless lazy people. In fact, God hates laziness. The first instruction that was ever given to man was to work.

"And every plant of the field before it was in the earth, and every herb of the field before it grew: for the LORD God had not caused it to rain upon the earth, and there was not a man to till the ground. **And the LORD God took the man, and put him into the Garden of Eden to dress it and keep it"** (Genesis 2:5, 15).

Man's first assignment on earth was to work. Work wasn't a punishment. I have heard a lot of people say God punished man to work after the disobedience but we realize from Genesis chapter 2 that long before the disobedience, man was mandated to till the ground.

Whatever you find yourself doing, give it your all if you are looking to win. That's the trade-off to win. Winners don't laze about at work and expect to be great.

Work and you will be satisfied with plenty so you can give to others.

DAY 28

"The only limit to our realization of tomorrow is the doubts of today"

Franklin D. Roosevelt; 32nd U.S. President.

Doubt kills many dreams. When we begin to believe in the possibility of our dreams we will face barriers. These barriers usually start in our minds; they all originate in our minds even before they manifest physically. We need to overcome them mentally before we do physically.

Doubt limits the possibility of our dreams. You need to overcome the doubt and to believe that our dreams are possible. Once you imbibe this belief, it becomes the fuel that propels you to overcome the barriers on the journey to the vision. When there is doubt, there is no way you can achieve your dream. As Brian Adams opined, ""*Thoughts of doubt and fear are pathways to failure*".

It is common to doubt your dreams and aspirations. We have so many reasons to doubt and discount our dreams in the face of our past and everything that is not in our favour. Where we come from, whether our parents have money or not, our race, the school we attended, when the odds are against us, etc.

When we begin to consider what's possible based on some of these factors, we limit how much we can do. Like we have discussed earlier in this book, we need to make use of our imagination. Our imagination is limitless.

DAY 29

"It wasn't raining when Noah built the ark."

Howard Ruff; Financial Adviser.

Noah, in the Bible was asked by God to build an ark because there was going to be a big flood. He had to build an ark when there was no weather report substantiating the fact that there will be a big flood. Noah went ahead to build the ark with everyone laughing and calling him crazy.

We often have to prepare for things we have no physical proof for if we are looking to accomplish great things. We also need this faith in pursuit of our dreams.

Preparation, even when nothing seems to be going your way is the highest proof of faith in your dream. You can't jump into the arena to compete when you haven't prepared. Preparation for something you don't see is the highest proof of faith. Don't wait for physical proofs before you take a step. Those who wait for favourable weather to sow always miss their sowing time and consequently reap no harvest. You can't expect everything to be favourable before you take the step. The people you see at the top started from somewhere. To get there you have to start climbing. It begins with a step; the first step.

What are you doing today with regards to your dream? Don't wait for proof to begin, believe in your dream regardless of whether it looks like possible or not.

DAY 30

"Human beings can alter their lives by
altering their attitudes of mind."

William James; Philosopher.

Isn't that wonderful? That a person can change his life just by changing their mindset. The moment you don't like the results you are seeing in your life, it is time to go back to your mind and make some changes.

You don't need to make big changes to make changes in your life. You only need to alter your mindset.

Begin to realize that you can develop a new perspective about your situation and the moment you think in that direction, your life is on a new tangent.

DAY 31

"Only those who risk going too far can possibly find out how far one can go."

T. S. Elliot; Essayist & Playwright.

When you can push yourself beyond the pain, when you can drag yourself once it gets difficult to move, you will realize that you carry more power in you than you ever thought.

When we don't risk, we will never know what could and would have happened. We need to push ourselves beyond what we know we can do before we can do what we didn't know we could do.

Don't operate in the confines of the normal, challenge yourself to get out of your comfort zone and go the extra mile for the extra is the difference between the ordinary and the extraordinary.

If you are doing what you know you can do then you are probably not pushing yourself enough. I didn't know I could do what I am doing now but I pushed myself and then I realized I had what it takes.

You have to push yourself beyond what's possible to reach the impossible.

SEPTEMBER

Welcome to the 9th month. This is the last month in the third quarter of the year. I believe that we have goals for this month.

Let's us begin to work towards our goal with enthusiasm. Continue to believe.

DAY 1

"No man is free who is not master to himself."

Epictetus; Philosopher.

Self-mastery is a skill and a habit we develop over time. If we commit to personal development and understanding of self, having control over our emotions and reactions, we reach a stage of self-mastery.
If external factors determine your emotions and reactions or actions, you are under the control of external factors and you are never free.

Commit to gaining control over yourself which includes developing strong self-discipline in your life.

Commit to becoming your best, gaining control over your emotions, your life and your daily activities. You can be free when you master yourself.

DAY 2

"Concentrated thoughts produce desired results."

Zig Ziglar; Author; Salesman and Motivational Speaker.

The greatest threat to success in our age is the amount of distraction we have in our media.

Our agenda these days is about doing a little bit of everything and never becoming great at anything. You find young people jumping from one vocation to the other because we are looking for a quick fix.
Our minds are cluttered with different kinds of ideas but we never get to focus on making any one of them work.

To achieve anything worthwhile, there is the need to concentrate our thought on one idea and focus on making it happen.

It is better to be 100% at one idea instead of being 25% at 4 ideas.
Go out today with one thing you would want to accomplish by the end of the year and something you need to get done before the year ends.
Concentrate your thoughts. Stop spreading yourself thin.

DAY 3

"Smooth seas do not make skillful sailors."

African proverb

Don't run away from the challenges coming along in your life. When you face and overcome them, it strengthens your resolve and makes you better.

If you want to live a great life, don't expect it to be without challenges. Great sailors have endured tumultuous waters and encountered great danger at sea. Those who succeed are those who overcome the challenge.

If you are looking to go through life smoothly without any serious waves beating your boat, you are not looking to be a skillful and a great sailor.

The more challenges you endure, the greater your skills become.
Today, as you step out, endure the waves, navigate around the big storms and remember that, with every challenge you overcome, you are developing a great skill for succeeding in life.

DAY 4

"Perseverance is the hard work you do after you get tired of doing the hard work you already did."

Newt Gingrich; Former Speaker of the U.S. House of Representatives.

After you have given 200%, then you have to give a 100% more. The one who really wants to win, goes the extra mile.

Don't look at the task, don't look at the obstacles and think you can't do it. When you take your eyes off your dreams, you get distracted. Your dreams should be your focus and keep you going not the challenges.

Don't stop because you got tired. Go beyond your pain and you will get the reward. What do you do when you get tired?

I love what Muhammad Ali said when a journalist asked him;

"How many sits-ups do you do in a day?"

Ali looked and answered;

"I don't really know because I only start counting when it starts burning and I am tired".

There are times you don't have to count the cost because it might scare you. There were days when I felt like who was really going to read this, I could just stop and no one would have ever known I was working on such a book.

I had stopped myself for days and weeks only to pick the script up again to go back to work on it. I just couldn't give it up. I had doubts, I had fears, really big ones, I was aware of how hard it was going to be but I also knew I carry this vision and I had to manifest it regardless. I knew there are many out there waiting to be inspired by this book.

DAY 5

"Talent is cheaper than table salt. What separates the talented individual from the successful one is a lot of hard work."

Stephen King; Author.

Everyone is talented to do something, few are disciplined to put in the work to get it done. Many believe that they can either get away with talent or people who succeed do so mainly because they are talented.
I may be talented to write but it doesn't just happen because I am talented. There is a lot of hard work needed to make it happen.
You may see it to be easy but it is not.

If are looking to succeed at anything, be willing to put in the work.

There is no way around hard work. Talent is never enough. Whatever your talents are, commit to working hard on yourself and becoming the best at your craft. That is when success will come to you.

DAY 6

"Luck is a dividend of sweat. The more you sweat, the luckier you get."

Ray Kroc; Businessman.

I have never believed in luck, I make my own luck.
When opportunity meets preparation, we call it luck.
Go out today and put in the work as we talked about
yesterday. Don't wait around waiting to step on gold or get
lucky with some lottery numbers.

If you walk around hoping something good happens to you,
you will hope and wish for the rest of your life. You have to
be willing to put in the work required to get lucky.

It takes a lot of hard work to get lucky. Let this be in your
mind and remember that when we put in the work, then we
shall win, maybe not immediately but definitely.

DAY 7

> "Do not let what you cannot do interfere with
> what you can do."

John Wooden; Basketball Player.

The time is far spent. Perhaps you have put off a lot of things because you thought you cannot do them. There is nothing like impossible. Again, wherever the word impossible exists is a sign of ignorance or limited knowledge.
Maybe you can't write but you can paint. Go ahead and paint.

Perhaps you can paint on canvas but not on the wall, paint on canvas. Why worry about what you can't do when there is plenty you can do?
You can't sing but you can dance, well, dance.

Go out today and do what you can do, forget about what you can't do. There is no time to waste.

DAY 8

"One sound idea is all that you need to achieve success."

Napoleon Hill; Author.

Someone said ideas are like seeds, there are lots of them out there but many of them don't grow into anything.
Does it mean you have to sit around and wait for that single idea that will change your life?

No, you go out there, try different ideas. Fail, try again. Get more ideas for you never know which one will be that idea which will set your life on a different path.

Let's go out today and never stop generating ideas, maybe the next one is the world's big idea.

DAY 9

"Our power is in our ability to decide."

Buckminster Fuller; Architect.

Making a decision is such a powerful thing many take for granted. There are times when we merely follow laid down creed thinking it is our own decisions.

If a man decides to accomplish something, the foundation of it is the clarity of the decision. When you know exactly what you want and determined to get it, then you have all the power to get there.

This decision making requires time and insight into what we want long term not short term. Our life is ruled by decisions we make every day.

Harness this power of decision making today, do not lease your decision-making power to anyone.

DAY 10

"If you can't fly, then run, if you can't run then walk, if you can't walk then crawl, but whatever you do you have to keep moving forward."

Martin Luther King Jr.; Civil Rights Activist.

There are times we know very well we have to move forward but we are stopped in our tracks afraid to take the first step. Our dreams may be a long shot away but we will only hit it if we keep shooting.

Whatever your goal is, whatever the dream is, it is the daily persistence steps we take which bring us closer to our destination. However difficult it gets, you can rest but don't quit---keep moving.

There is no more time for excuses. Don't hold yourself back. You can rest, you can re-evaluate and strategize for your next step but keep moving.

Commit to your dreams. The most important thing is to know where you are going, Dr. King had a dream and that was what he was fighting for. If we consider him as a man like us, then this motivates us to go out there to also make our dreams possible.

He was reiterating something I believe in **"direction is much more important than speed"**. So, the only way to succeed at the dream you are following is to keep going.

You are not looking to get farther; you are looking to finish.

Hebrews 12:1b- "…and let us run with patience the race that is set before us".

Your race is set before you. The goal is to finish, don't be trapped into trying to finish ahead of someone.

If you can run; then run, if you can walk; please keep walking; if you have to crawl; get on your knees and start crawling; whatever happens you have to finish your race. How you get there is not the focus; either by running, walking or crawling, be patient, just keep moving.

Dr. King kept persisting, he kept moving forward even to the point of death. Determine in your heart, I will persist till I succeed.

Don't worry if others are running, your friend started a business so you also have to start a business? If that is your motivation then you are poorly motivated. Find your own reasons why you want to do it.

I may be crawling but I know where I am going and I will get there. It will be more satisfying at the end if I followed and achieved my dreams and never felt pressured to do what others are doing.

Imbibe this idea, never give up. Don't worry about the pace, you may have wished to see results soon but don't stop. Keep going, run, walk, and crawl, whatever you have to do, most importantly keep moving forward.

DAY 11

"Energy and persistence conquer all things"

Benjamin Franklin; Founding Father of the United States.

Benjamin Franklin is a hero of mine. I wrote this quote down and found myself meditating on it.

Most of the failures we have in the world are people who get tired easily and have no desire to keep going. They stop when they are tired, they lose their enthusiasm and energy every time they have a task at hand. They get tired reading, they get tired writing, they get tired training, they get tired working, always tired.

To succeed at anything, you have to develop the **love, enthusiasm and energy** to keep going when everyone else is giving up. Don't stop because you are tired, stop when you are done and get reward for it. The Akan's of Ghana have a saying "edwuma sen nnyi akotua", literally meaning "half work done doesn't get a reward". Get committed, stay on it, and finish it.

Don't panic in the face of adversity, keep persisting. The wind wears the rock not because it is stronger but because it persists. In all you do, please know that without the energy and enthusiasm, you will surely give up. Never be indolent in any venture you find yourself in. Build yourself up for something bigger.

DO it for your future, resolve to persist till you succeed.

DAY 12

"A little more persistence, a little more effort and what seemed hopeless failure may turn to a glorious success"

Elbert Hubbard; Writer, Artist & Philosopher.

When the woman in the delivery room is told to push a little more, it is not because it is not painful, it is because the next push only brings her baby closer to coming into the world.

When the pain gets unbearable and she is about giving up, she is told to give one more push. It is painful, its crushes but if she does push, she will hear the cry of her baby.

In life, you get to a point which seems like a woman in labour. You are in pain, everything is falling apart, and nothing seems to work. If only you will try just one more time, you will give another push, you will try another shot, you will just hold on and not give up, just a little more, you will win.

When you feel like giving up, ask yourself why you started in the first place. Thomas Edison said "most of the world's failures are people who didn't know how close they were to success when they gave up". When you are tired, when you are frustrated, when you want to give up, just tell yourself "Just a little more".

Don't give up yet, study one more hour, train one more hour, read one more book. Every shot you take brings you closer to the next home run. Don't stop now, you have come too far to give up, just a little more time. Hold on!

DAY 13

"Ambition is the path to success. Persistence is the vehicle you arrive in."

Bill Bradley; Former American Senator.

I was on YouTube during the Christmas holidays to look for a message on AMBITION. I typed the word "ambition" in the search bar, I downloaded one titled "THE POWER OF AMBITION by JIM ROHN which was an audiobook.

I was enriched by that message as I laid down all night listening to the 6 and half hour audio book. I learned that without ambition, there is no starting point for success. You can accomplish anything based on your ambition.

"Ambition is a powerful force. The power of ambition turns hopeful wishes into reality. It leads you on a good course to the good life. Legitimate ambition says I only want something at the service of others not at the expense of others. If it is your ambition to be great you must first find a way to do so by serving others, if it is your ambition to be wealthy, you must first learn how to give, if it is your ambition to be healthy, you must first learn to stop doing the things that can make you and others sick"-Jim Rohn

What is your desire? What are you reaching for? You may share your goals with some friends and they tell you that you "are over ambitious". Change the people in your circle, choose like-minded friends. Negative people can destroy your ambition. Surround yourself with equally ambitious people.

You may have a great desire to help the world, invent something wonderful, build a lasting business but you will soon realize that it is not enough. Just the desire to succeed won't bring you success, there will be challenges and you have to overcome with persistence.

Go out there and start travelling the road to success, be determined but remember that, the path is not always smooth, there will be challenges, there will be setbacks, you may fail, but the vehicle you are travelling in is persistence. Ride on!

Woody Hayes says "paralyze resistance with persistence". To arrive at success, you need to nurture a great ambition and then resolve not to give up regardless of the opposition. Go for what you desire and never give up.

DAY 14

"If you're going through hell, keep going"

Winston Churchill; Former British Prime Minister.

We are presented with challenges in life all the time. Life is not all sunshine and rainbow, there are strong winds, storms, hurricanes, earthquakes and tornadoes.

Life is hard, sometimes it's a mess regardless of your age, it's a melee as everyone finds out at a point. How you deal with it is what defines your future. We should all realize that each passerby has a life as vivid and complex as our own.

Our problems are similar, it's our solutions which make the difference. Some give up, others don't!

This may enervate you, this may force you to stop midway as you pursue your goals. You had bad grades in school, you failed in business, you made a mistake, you missed an opportunity, you applied for a spot and you were denied, it's hard.

It's hard handling the tragedies of life. You may lose loved ones, it's rough. You may lose at a point when you've done everything right, it's humiliating, it's frustrating but until you go through it you will never understand why it happened.

We go through stages in life when we momentarily have no idea what's going on. The caterpillar needs to go through a transition and lose itself in order to turn into a different organism, more beautiful and majestic called the butterfly.

When metamorphosis begins, the caterpillar never understands why. As humans, we go through our own metamorphosis, we encounter our own challenges, "it is like riding the bicycle, you have to keep going to keep your balance", as Einstein said.

No matter what happens, get up and try again. Keep going, in the end you will understand that it was only preparing you for something greater. It was building your capacity and tenacity. That's life. You have to pass all your tests to become the best.

Never stop walking even if you are going through hell.

DAY 15

"Patience, persistence and perspiration make an unbeatable combination for success."

Napoleon Hill; Author.

Many people are looking for secrets to success, over the years it has been increasingly clear that there is no secret. All the cards are bare on the table, but many fail to make the commitment.

Hard work, patience, ambition, commitment, discipline, consistency and persistence are all ingredients for success.

Thomas Edison said "genius is 1% inspiration and 99% perspiration". Reading Napoleon's quote, you understand that persistence and hard work is inevitable if you want to succeed at anything.

You have to perspire, you have to work hard at it. You should understand that when you start working on your dreams, you won't immediately get results. You will have to be patient.

Never be in a hurry to achieve something great, great things take time. Rome was not built in a day but they started building from the scratch. Never be disappointed when you don't get answers from the beginning, persist. Never lose hope, don't give up, be patient and keep on working on your dreams.

Patience in this fast-paced world is a great virtue, many people are rushing to get to the top. Don't be in a hurry to get to the arena. Take the time to practice, work at it, make mistakes, get better and never be afraid to try and don't stop because you made a mistake. It's hard, easy is not an option. Life on its own is hard, we all have our individual experiences. If you give up easily then you will never know how far you can go in life.

"If thou faint in the day of adversity, thy strength is small"- King Solomon (Proverbs 24:5). Persist, be patient and keep working hard every day. Don't rush to the arena to compete, take the time to keep improving, be patient, and get better till you master every skill.

If you don't give up, if you keep working, if you persist even in the face of adversities, I assure you that you will succeed.

DAY 16

"Those at the top of the mountain didn't fall there."

Marcus Washling;

That's pretty obvious right? Not so. We often feel like the "successful" * in life became successful overnight. Like the great comedian just became a great comedian overnight, the great football players woke up one day and became great.

We are not previewed to their struggles, to the times when they had to wake up at dawn to train, to work hard. Time in the gym, the media won't show us that. All we see is the public glory so we are made to think everything just happens.

We see mountain climbers when they are at the top of the mountain. We don't see them climb, remember, they didn't fall there.
Keep climbing your own mountain.

- * Whatever success means to you.

DAY 17

"I made a resolve then that I was going to amount to something if I could. And no hours, nor amount of labor, nor amount of money would deter me from giving the best that there was in me. And I have done that ever since, and I win by it. I know."

Harlan Sanders, Founder of Kentucky Fried Chicken

I don't need to tell you the story of KFC. But reading this quote from him should make you write down the same resolution.

I wish to emphasize the personal pronoun in the sentence; "I" am going to amount to something.

Decide to make the commitment to the resolution that you will become what you have determined in your heart.

It doesn't matter how long it takes, how many days, weeks, months or years it takes, how much money and energy you have to invest, you're going to see it through.

It takes grit and a determination keep working on this commitment to making something out of your life.

Let this be your oath to life.

DAY 18

"I don't quit; I only change my plans."

George Weir; President, Tomorrows' Stars &
Engineering Consultant

This is from my mentor. George Weir, was in Ghana for a business trip which turned into a huge opportunity because he saw the potential in a kid he met. He started an NGO to help make education possible in a Ghanaian community. He is now the President and Founder of a thriving NGO helping brilliant but needy students get education in Elmina, Ghana.

The NGO has the tagline, "making education possible", training young people to help other young people in the community under a project known as "paying it forward". You can read more about him and the NGO's work here: www.tstars.org.

We were having a conversation one day when he made this statement. As always, I wrote it down. I love collecting quotes.

He never quits he only changes his plans. I have made this my resolution too. Change the plan not the goal.

If your plan doesn't go well, change it but don't quit. Change the plan, not the purpose.

DAY 19

"It doesn't take any effort to stay at the bottom of the sea, just allow yourself to drown but to stay at the top you have to swim every day. It requires daily relentless pursuit to stay on top of your dreams. It is easy to be ordinary, if you're looking to be extraordinary, you have to put in the extra work"

Rudolph Mensah, Author & Speaker

It's so easy to be ordinary. It takes a lot of hard work to be extraordinary. It's easy to go along the well-worn path.

If you are looking for a "safe life" or a life without any commitment then you are free to just drift along with the masses.
If you are looking to make a difference or make an impact in the world, then you have to go against the status quo. You have to be willing to go against the tide.

I have chosen to stay on top and this means striving to be my best every day. Going against the obstacles and facing challenges every day.

So, what is going to be?

On top of the sea or you want to drop to the bottom of the sea with 90% of the population?

DAY 20

"When the blind leads the blind, they both fall in a ditch"

Jesus Christ of Nazareth; The Son of God.

Leadership is an essential element in life. Who you follow determines how far you get in life.
We may be where we are because of what we were told, what we learned, the kind of teachers we had, what we learned growing up.

It is important to decide who you listen to. The kind of tapes you listen, the kind of preachers you listen to, the books you read, these things determine who is leading you.

In your finances, personal development, spiritual development, career development, etc., who is leading you?

I have this question for you today, who are you following?

DAY 21

"I'm a big believer in the power of inexperience. It was the greatest asset I had when I started TFA. If I had known at the outset how hard it was going to be, I might never have started.

Wendy Kopp; CEO of Teach for America.

Sometimes a level of uncertainty is necessary in leading us to the success we seek. When we get to the point where we know all the limitations and the risk involved, we often tend not to venture into certain areas of life because we are aware of the fact and therefore predict the outcome.

To do something extraordinary, you often need to be blinded by the fact and only go with your instinct.
According to the law of aerodynamics, the bumblebee isn't flight worthy because of its structure and wings but the bumblebee flies anyway.

Why? The bumblebee isn't aware of these laws of physics. Often what stops us from getting to our dream is what we know to be possible and not possible. Learn to marry your intellect with your instinct.

Allow yourself to go in without hesitation. Sometimes, don't try to be too clever. Listen to your brain but follow your heart.

DAY 22

"Our patience will achieve more than our force"

Edmund Burke; Stateman.

There is an old African proverb which says "the day a mosquito lands on your testicles is the day you will realize that you can't solve every problem with violence."

Patience is a virtue and weak people don't have patience. It takes a strong person to be patient. To wait. To be still. To continue working for something which is yet to happen.

Many will fidget, break down, give in because of the frustration which comes with waiting.

Don't force it, give yourself some time, keep working, you shall be rewarded. We shall win, maybe not immediately but definitely.

DAY 23

"Age is not a question of years. The years may wrinkle your skin but it is the lack of interest that wrinkles your soul"

General Douglas McArthur; Five Star General & Field Marshall.

Nothing is ever interesting if you are not interested. What you enjoy is what you invest your energy into.
You won't be tired by age, you will be tired by your lack of enthusiasm. A man at 78 who enjoys reading will still enjoy reading.

A pianist who loves to play will play at 90 even with fine tremors.
Someone once said, some people die at 25 and only get buried at 75.

Don't let boredom and lack of enthusiasm wrinkle your soul. Every day, go out there with new zeal and energy in your day.

We can't avoid growing old, but we can do it in style.

DAY 24

"I have learned silence from the talkative, tolerance from the intolerant, and kindness from the unkind, yet strange, I am ungrateful to those teachers"

Khalil Gibran (from his book: Sand and Form)

Life has a way of teaching us basic principles. Anything we see out there that we abhor has a way of teaching us something in ourselves.

I have always vowed I wasn't going to be what I saw growing up. I am the kind of person I am today because I saw how my Uncle struggled with his life as a school drop-out and a man who never invested in himself.

I saw how fast a man can fall from grace to grass as my father descended low in his life due to wrong decisions.

Sometimes, the examples we see may not be the best but they have a way of teaching us how not to live our lives.

Today, as you go out remember you should pay attention and learn from what's going on around you. You don't have to go down the same path which has led many to destruction.

DAY 25

"As a child, my mum always told me; whatever you are doing, wherever you are, may it be said of you that because you were there things were better"

Rudolph Mensah, Author & Speaker

This has been my personal principle and philosophy in life. This is my life vision. It doesn't matter what I am doing or where I am, my goal in life is to make a difference by being different.

What is your mission statement in life?

If you don't have one, write one today and measure your daily performance with it at the end of the day.

When I get home at night, how do I know I had a good day? I ask myself:

Did I make someone's life better? Did I make a small difference in someone's life? Was it better because I was there?

If I answer yes to even the smallest difference I made, then I had a good day because that's my life mission statement.

If I am there, things should be better.

What's yours?

DAY 26

"When we are no longer able to change a situation, we are challenged to change ourselves."

Viktor E. Frankl; Man's Search for Meaning

If you want to change anything in the world, change yourself first. Don't focus on what's outside of you, look inside of you and begin to look at what you can do differently.

Newton's law of motion states that "every action requires an equal and opposite reaction". So, if you are looking to see a change or change the results or reaction you get in your life, focus on something different. Put in a different action.

Focus on changing yourself. Focus on the positives and you will realize that things around you will change.

Become the person who can cause changes, don't focus on changing the things around you, be involved in changing yourself.

Only then will you be in the position to change your world.

DAY 27

Plato;

"No matter how old you are now. You are never too young or too old for success or going after what you want. Here's a short list of people who accomplished great things at different ages:

---

1) Helen Keller, at the age of 19 months, became deaf and blind. But that didn't stop her. She was the first deaf and blind person to earn a Bachelor of Arts degree.

2) Mozart was already competent on keyboard and violin; he composed from the age of 5.

3) Shirley Temple was 6 when she became a movie star on "Bright Eyes."

4) Anne Frank was 12 when she wrote the diary of Anne Frank.

5) Magnus Carlsen became a chess Grandmaster at the age of 13.

6) Nadia Comăneci was a gymnast from Romania that scored seven perfect 10.0 and won three gold medals at the Olympics at age 14.

7) Tenzin Gyatso was formally recognized as the 14th Dalai Lama in November 1950, at the age of 15.

8) Pele, a soccer superstar, was 17 years old when he won the world cup in 1958 with Brazil.

9) Elvis was a superstar by age 19.

10) John Lennon was 20 years and Paul McCartney was 18 when the Beatles had their first concert in 1961.

11) Jesse Owens was 22 when he won 4 gold medals in Berlin 1936.

12) Beethoven was a piano virtuoso by age 23

13) Isaac Newton wrote Philosophiæ Naturalis Principia Mathematica at age 24

14) Roger Bannister was 25 when he broke the 4 minute mile record

15) Albert Einstein was 26 when he wrote the theory of relativity

16) Lance E. Armstrong was 27 when he won the tour de France

17) Michelangelo created two of the greatest sculptures "David" and "Pieta" by age 28

18) Alexander the Great, by age 29, had created one of the largest empires of the ancient world

19) J.K. Rowling was 30 years old when she finished the first manuscript of Harry Potter

20) Amelia Earhart was 31 years old when she became the first woman to fly solo across the Atlantic Ocean

21) Oprah was 32 when she started her talk show, which has become the highest-rated program of its kind

22) Edmund Hillary was 33 when he became the first man to reach Mount Everest

23) Martin Luther King Jr. was 34 when he wrote the speech "I Have a Dream."

24) Marie Curie was 35 years old when she got nominated for a Nobel Prize in Physics

25) The Wright brothers, Orville (32) and Wilbur (36) invented and built the world's first successful airplane and making the first controlled, powered and sustained heavier-than-air human flight

26) Vincent Van Gogh was 37 when he died virtually unknown, yet his paintings today are worth millions.

27) Neil Armstrong was 38 when he became the first man to set foot on the moon.

28) Mark Twain was 40 when he wrote "The Adventures of Tom Sawyer", and 49 years old when he wrote "Adventures of Huckleberry Finn"

29) Christopher Columbus was 41 when he discovered the Americas

30) Rosa Parks was 42 when she refused to obey the bus driver's order to give up her seat to make room for a white passenger

31) John F. Kennedy was 43 years old when he became President of the United States

32) Henry Ford Was 45 when the Ford T came out.

33) Suzanne Collins was 46 when she wrote "The Hunger Games"

34) Charles Darwin was 50 years old when his book On the Origin of Species came out.

35) Leonardo Da Vinci was 51 years old when he painted the Mona Lisa.

36) Abraham Lincoln was 52 when he became president.

37) Ray Kroc Was 53 when he bought the McDonalds Franchise and took it to unprecedented levels.

38) Dr. Seuss was 54 when he wrote "The Cat in the Hat".

40) Chesley "Sully" Sullenberger III was 57 years old when he successfully ditched US Airways Flight 1549 in the Hudson River in 2009. All of the 155 passengers aboard the aircraft survived

41) Colonel Harland Sanders was 61 when he started the KFC Franchise

42) J.R.R Tolkien was 62 when the Lord of the Ring books came out

43) Ronald Reagan was 69 when he became President of the US

44) Jack Lalane at age 70 handcuffed, shackled, towed 70 rowboats

45) Nelson Mandela was 76 when he became President

Need I say more? No, go out today and become your dream regardless of your age.

DAY 28

"The greatest things you intend to do some time must have a beginning if they are ever to be done, so begin to do something worthwhile today"

Grenville Kleiser; Author.

Yesterday, we saw a list of people who overcame the barrier of age and obstacles on their way to becoming great. Did they wait forever? No.

Get off your seat today and begin working on your dream. Don't wait till everything comes together. Everything won't come together.

I have said if you have 65-75% assurance of what you want to do, go ahead. A level of uncertainty is necessary to keep you going.
The year still has a lot of days before we end it. What is it you want to do?

Begin today. Not tomorrow. Today. Right now. Close the book and get to work.

DAY 29

"Live your truth. Express your love. Share your enthusiasm. Take action towards your dreams. Walk your talk. Dance and sing to your music. Embrace your blessings. Make today worth remembering."

Steve Maraboli; Unapologetically You: Reflections on Life and the Human Experience

What is your truth? What's your life guiding principle? Few days ago, I spoke about my life mission as making things better wherever I am.
This is my truth, this is my measure of how well I will live on earth. I believe in making others better.

Express your love. Love to me is action, not mere words. Tell people how much they mean to you but most importantly show them. Don't just talk about it, express it. Everyday. Spread love, the world will do with lots of love.
Again, do I keep it to myself? No. I am talking to people about, writing about it, sharing my enthusiasm. Share your enthusiasm, don't let others infect you with negativity. Spread your enthusiasm.

Then, take action, I have talked about taking action a lot. This is because that is the bridge between just having a dream and making it happen. After you read today's quote, what you do with it is the important thing. Take action.
Go out and practice what you preach, dance, have some fun and be happy with the blessings of life. Go out today and make it a masterpiece.

DAY 30

"The problem, often not discovered until late in life, is that when you look for things in life like love, meaning, motivation, it implies they are sitting behind a tree or under a rock. The most successful people in life recognize, that in life they create their own love, they manufacture their own meaning, they generate their own motivation. For me, I am driven by two main philosophies, know more today about the world than I knew yesterday. And lessen the suffering of others. You'd be surprised how far that gets you."

Neil deGrasse Tyson; Astrophysicist.

Simply, take responsibility for your own life. Don't look for happiness, love, meaning and motivation from external sources.
If you derive these things from the outside, you will always end up being disappointed.

We seek without what is within. Take this profound advice and own your happiness and find your motivation.

Take this advice, one, know more than you knew yesterday and two, lesson other people's suffering. This will bring you a sense of fulfilment.

OCTOBER

Welcome to the 10th month.

We are getting closer to the end of the year.

I encourage you to keep working on your dreams.

See you at the top.

DAY 1

"All great achievements require time."

Maya Angelou; Poet, Singer, Memoirist, and Civil Rights Activist.

Nothing great ever happens suddenly. If you are looking to succeed at anything great, be prepared to put in the work and be patient.

Trust the process and allow the process of time to make it happen.
We live in era where technology has made everything faster so we tend to believe we can achieve anything overnight.

You can't download success, it requires commitment and a process of grit.
Are you committed long-term or you just kind of want it overnight?

DAY 2

"When defeat comes, accept it as a signal that your plans are not sound, rebuild those plans, and set sail once more toward your coveted goal."

Napoleon Hill; Author: Think and Grow Rich.

One thing you have to understand here is that, sometimes when you are failing repeatedly at something you have to sit back and make an honest assessment, "is this is for me?". Sometimes failure is a feedback, get the signal and not the noise. What is it teaching you and what can you learn?

You see, there are times when failure could be a feedback that this is not the way you should go.

This is the reason why failure is an important ingredient for success. Find out if you can change the plan or modify your goals. Not giving up doesn't mean you keep doing the same thing over and over again knowing fully well your plan isn't working. Change the plan but not the goal.

When I say learn from your failures, it doesn't mean that you do that and keep doing the same thing over and over again, that is synonymous to insanity.

Now, rebuild your strategy and let's go out today and begin again.

DAY 3

"If you have a dream, don't just sit there. Gather courage to believe that you can succeed and leave no stone unturned to make it a reality."

Dr. Roopleen; Author.

Commitment is the key to becoming your dream. You can't just kind of want it, you must commit fully to making it happen. Taking action on your dream is the only way you can make it a reality.

First, you need to believe that you can become your dream. Your dream is possible. You first have to believe that and say it to yourself every day. It is not only important but necessary.

This new idea of believing your dream is possible gives you a renewed sense of hope. The hope to begin the journey to greatness. This reconditions your mind and sets you on a new path to success.

"If you don't believe it, you can't achieve it".

Why is it important to believe your dreams are possible? This helps you to imagine the future you dream of. Until you can imagine what your dream looks like, you can't become it.

The imagination helps you to look beyond the current pain and see the possibility of your dreams. Imagination is **"images** from another **nation**"; the nation you are striving to get to. Imagine it; envision it. When obstacles show up, the imagination gives you insight into the future and therefore takes you beyond the pain.

Be positive, be resilient, believe it is possible even when everyone says it is impossible. Don't let anything stop you. Believe that it doesn't matter the size of your dream, it is possible! Believe.

DAY 4

"Many of life's noblest enterprises might never have been undertaken if all the difficulties and defects could be foreseen"

Theodore L. Cuyler; Writer.

If I knew how hard it was going to be to start building myself into an author, I would have settled into my profession and just stayed in my corner.

If you know how hard it was going to be, you probably wouldn't have started the business or gone to college.

Many of the great inventions and business we see were started when the founders had no idea what's next or the obstacles on the way.

Deal with them as they come. Don't be so bogged down with the details. Take the first step in faith and keep going.

DAY 5

"To be successful you must accept all challenges that come your way. You can't just accept the ones you like."

Mike Gafka;

If you only do the things you are comfortable with, then you can never challenge yourself out of the ordinary. You will settle for the normal.

There is the natural tendency to be selective with the challenges and projects we undertake. We are not looking to suffer, we are not looking to be embarrassed so we only accept the things we know we can handle and pass on the difficult tasks to others. What we forget is that, the bigger the obstacle, the bigger the reward. The bigger the challenge, the bigger the results you get by solving it.

If you are looking to solve a problem for a hundred people, you only get rewarded for a 100. Do it for a thousand or a million, you will get reward for a thousand or a million respectively.

So, don't always go for the easy task, challenge yourself and embrace the seemingly impossible once. When you succeed, you will be happy and more confident, when you fail, you tried, you learn your lessons and you are well equipped to try again and this time wiser.

DAY 6

"Take up one idea. Make that one idea your life--think of it, dream of it, live on that idea. Let the brain, muscles, nerves, every part of your body, be full of that idea, and just leave every other idea alone. This is the way to success."

Swami Vivekananda; Monk.

What is that single idea you will dedicate your life to? What one thing will you do if success was guaranteed? If you knew you wouldn't fail, what is that one thing you will dedicate your life to achieving? Write down ten things you would like to achieve in your lifetime. Look at them carefully, if you were given all the resources you need, all the support, the knowledge and the required environment to work, which one of these ten things will you give your life to?

Write down that one idea. Think about it, imagine it, let your whole life be about making that idea happen.
When you are fully concentrated on this single idea, you will realize that everything you do will be in the direction of this idea and things will begin to align in that direction.

First, you have to be able to define this idea for yourself and why it has meaning for you.

DAY 7

"The will to win is worthless if you do not have the will to prepare."

Louis Pasteur; Biologist.

Preparation is key to any successful venture. Athletes who are looking to win gold medals don't go into a race unprepared. Students who expecting to excel in their examinations don't go into the examination room unprepared.

Your dream may require you to attend evening school to get you prepared. Do it. You may have to go to college, get the education. You may need technical training; you have to enroll in a fashion school? Well, get in and start learning.

If we don't develop our abilities, we can't survive in this fast-changing world. It is not just what you can do but how well you can do it.
On WikiHow, I have read a lot about writing, blogging, speaking and publishing. I have read a great deal of articles about writing and publishing a book.

I have joined various "author groups" on the internet; I have social alliances with people who are doing what I want to do. I follow authors and I learn. Without preparation, you are setting yourself up to fail.

DAY 8

"The greatest things ever done on earth have been done little by little"

Thomas Guthrie; Revered Minister & Philanthropist.

You don't have to get over it in one leap, sometimes and mostly to get anywhere worthwhile, you have to be willing to put in the work and trust the process, believing in the journey.

You need patience, now more than ever. We live in a fast-paced world where we are all looking to make some big impact overnight. We start something and we don't seem to make any impact in three months we stop and start doing something else.

We must develop the attitude of sticking-to-one-thing till we get it through. Find that one idea and don't be bothered by what others are doing. Don't ever rush or be in haste to get something done. Don't be lazy, work hard at it but be patient. Trust the process, little by little, it will happen.

DAY 9

"There are two types of people who will tell you that you cannot make a difference in this world: those who are afraid to try and those who are afraid you will succeed."

Ray Goforth; Executive Director, Society of Professional Employees in Aerospace

---

I have encountered both. It is always important to pay attention to what people are saying so you can hear what they are not saying.
The subtle intent of their careful warning about the impossibility of your dream.

I think no one knows enough to be a pessimist. What have you done, how long have you done it, how many times have you tried to come to the conclusion that something is not possible?

You can offer your opinion but never use absolute terms as descriptors. Never, impossible, these words change in the face of progressive knowledge and understanding.
When people are afraid of something they project their fears on you.

Again, there are those who don't want you to try because they feel you might succeed and rob them of their excuse for failure.

Don't let either of them disrupt your plans. Go and do what you have planned to do. Face your life.

DAY 10

"As a man thinketh in his heart so is he"

King Solomon (Proverbs 27:3a); King of Ancient Israel.

This is the single message motivational speakers and personal development authors have distilled in their speeches and books over the years.

Napoleon Hill in his book, THINK AND GROW RICH, is basically based on this profound truth.

Our thoughts control what we do and what we become. Do you think of yourself as a failure or a success?

Henry Ford added, "whether you think you can or you can't, you're right." This is very important in our pursuit of our dreams in life.

It hinges on your mindset. How you see yourself and what your belief system is. If you don't like what you see in your life, change how you think, what goes into your mind.

Control your thought and you can control your life.

DAY 11

"A ship in habour is safe…but that is not what ships are for"

John A. Shedd; Merchant.

If you don't climb you won't fall but what joy there is if you spend your whole life on the ground?

Ships are made for the high seas, not for the habour. You can decide to live your life in a small corner, away from taking any risk. You will be fed and maybe grow to be a 100-years but what a way to live?

Helen Keller said "life is a daring adventure or nothing else." In this era, not taking a risk is a big risk. So, go out there and sail your ship.

Catch some breeze, enjoy the waves and the scare of falling into the sea. Live your life and get to the end and say, "that was quite a ride."

DAY 12

"It's our choices, Harry, that show what we truly are, far more than our abilities"

Prof. Albus Dumbledore (Character in "Harry Porter" Movie)

Life is made up of choices. Little tiny choices we make every day determine the direction of our lives.

Daily decisions we make every day, choices we make every day determine the shape of our lives.

It is not talent which is central to what we can achieve but our choices.

Do we choose to try or do we choose to hold on? Do we go left or do we go right?

What I have realized over the years is that no choice is perfect. Not making a decision is a decision itself which is the worst decision you can make.

So, make a choice, look at the facts, listen to your instinct and marry your intellect with your instinct, come up with a choice. No decision is the best decision. You just have to make one. Go right and if you find out right is the wrong road, you can just turn left and you will be on the right road. Just don't stand there.

The next thing is to follow through and not be deterred no matter how hard it gets. Making a choice may be easy for some people but following through is the hardest part.

That shows who we truly are.

DAY 13

"Victory belongs to the most persevering"

Napoleon Bonaparte; Stateman & Military Leader.

Napoleon was a great warrior and conqueror. With his experience and many victories in wars, I find these words true from a man who won many wars because he persevered even against great odds.

There will be challenges, there will be obstacles, there will be opposition, but were you expecting it to be an easy ride?

The only way to win is go through it, around it, over it or under it. The point is, don't be stopped. Persevere.

Perseverance in the face of opposition is the key to overcoming obstacles and becoming victorious.

Are you going to quit because things got tough?

DAY 14

"The future belongs to those who prepare for it today"

Malcom X; Muslim Minister & Human Rights Activist.

The best preparation for tomorrow is doing your very best today.
What we do today, the investment we make today compounds to the result we get tomorrow.

The question is, how well are you preparing today? We have discussed how important preparation is in becoming successful in projects we undertake in our lives.

As you go through the day, make a deliberate determined and conscious effort to invest the time and energy into your life and work on becoming what you dream of.

Remember, the future belongs to those who prepare for it today. Today matters in how you live tomorrow. Don't mess it up.

DAY 15

"Everyone has a plan 'til they get punched in the mouth."

Mike Tyson; Retired Professional Boxer.

We stumble, we fall, we falter. We get punched in the face. We encounter challenges we didn't plan for.

What do we do when we get punched in the mouth?

You are allowed to rest to get your vision back. Find out what happened, understand the situation but don't wait too long. Keep moving.

Keep working and this time try to avoid the pitfalls. We can't' always predict what will happen and life sometimes catches us on the blind side but continue to believe you will get through it.

Believe in yourself and in your dream. Don't let your guard down or you get punched in the face again. Lots of people who succeed get punched in the mouth, several times. Be encouraged, you are in a good company.

Now, wipe your tears and let's go give it another shot.

DAY 16

"A man sooner or later discovers that he is the master-gardener of his soul, the director of his life"

James Allen; Philosophical writer, (1864-1912)

The question is, will it be sooner or later for you?

I came to this realization in my life when I got into junior high school, at a young age I understood the meaning of responsibility.

I had to make decisions, what I wanted to do with my life, which high school to attend and what program to study. In Ghana where I come from, high school students are required to choose a program of study, the sciences, the arts, the vocational and the technical.
Where you choose most likely becomes your path for life.

I have also seen many grow into an old age never realizing the fact that a man is the director of his own life. We blame the government, the society, our parents, we blame everyone else for our woes and inadequacies in life.
Until you accept this responsibility about your life being your own, you are bound to be blaming other people for your failures.
Own your life and commit to making it the best you can be.

DAY 17

"The opposite of courage in our society is not cowardice, it is conformity."

Rollo May; Existential Psychologist, (1909-1994)

We want to wear what everyone is wearing. We want to eat what everyone is eating. We want to do what everyone is doing.

Why?

Because we are afraid to be different. We are afraid to look different. We are afraid to be called names. So, we fight and do everything possible to be just like everyone else.

It is easy to fit in. you are not challenged to be any different. You don't have to worry about developing yourself. You can be like everyone else.
It takes courage to say I will pursue my dream. It takes courage to say against all odds I will try. It takes courage to say even though no one else has done it, I am going to give it my best shot.

When you don't have this courage, you settle in, you join the band wagon. You simply stand in line. So, I agree with Rollo, the opposite of courage isn't cowardice but conformity.

Everyone wants to be like everyone else.

DAY 18

"Fearlessness is like a muscle. I know from
my own life that the more I exercise it, the
more natural it becomes to not let my fears run
me.

Arianna Huffington; Author &
Businesswoman.

Do it today, become more confident to do it again tomorrow.
That's how you build confidence.

If you are always afraid to try or go out and do something you
are afraid of doing, you will always find yourself cowering and
never having the courage to go out there and do anything.

What are you hiding from? Life is full of risks. Everywhere
you go, life will get to you. You can be in the stands or on the
field and you will still get knocked down.

Someone once said, fear is the most destructive of all human
diseases. Begin by doing the little things you are afraid of
doing, do it today. Make that call, ask for the new chair in your
office, don't ask for the raise yet, start with the small things
and then finally you can ask for your raise or take that new
job.
Are you with me? Let's go out today and exercise our
confidence muscles.

DAY 19

"Everyone wants to live on top of the
mountain, but all the happiness and growth
occurs while you're climbing it."

Andy Rooney; Television Writer.

It is the process which is the most important. I am on a
journey and I am more excited about the journey than the
destination.
We see the summit and all we want is to get to the top of the
mountain.

We believe we will only be happy if we can get to the top of
the mountain. This is where we get it all wrong.
We don't celebrate when we get to the top, we celebrate all the
way.

We are not only happy when we get to the finish line, we are
happy with every step we take. In fact, there is no finish line.
It is the progressive realization of the dream which brings us
fulfilment.

Take some time to savour every step you take and be
encouraged that you will get to your destination.
Pay attention to the climb and who you become while you
climb, don't be drawn so much into focusing on the top. You
will one day find yourself at the top.

DAY 20

"Reading is a source of potency, become a walking encyclopedia of answers for anyone who has questions"

Tim Sanders; Author.

Do I agree? Absolutely. I have been reading since I could pronounce the word r-e-a-d. I was read to by my mum and my dad always made me read before I could get a pesewa to buy toffee.

I often have my friends asking me about things even stuff I didn't study in school because they know I read a lot.

I find it interesting that I happen to have a broad understanding of certain subjects even outside of my area of study. That's how potent you become when you read.

Reading opens up opportunities and you never know which one opportunity will open the door to your success.
So, find some time to read. Read what you are interested in, read a page, a paragraph.
Soon, you will realize that everything starts adding up. Read, it's the best you can do for yourself.

DAY 21

"Life is a series of problem-solving opportunities. The problems you face will either defeat you or develop you depending on how you respond to them."

Rick Warren; Pastor.

Don't run away from your problems. Embrace them. Find a way through them. Solve them. Don't back down.

Failure, someone said, defeats losers and inspires winners. These challenges coming in the form of problem-solving opportunities and when we embrace them, we bring out the best in us.

In the face of challenges, some people break down, others break records. Will you rise to the occasion or will you wither to the ground?

Will you run away from the challenge or will you stand and take the opportunity.

How are you going to respond to your problem-solving opportunities?

DAY 22

"The great thing in this world is not so much where you stand, as in what direction you are moving."

Oliver Wendell Holmes; Former Associate of the Supreme Court of the U.S.

If you don't know where you are going, how fast you run doesn't really matter. Life is always moving and when you don't know which direction you are going, then you are lost forever.

You can't stand at the crossroad forever in life not knowing where you are going. You have to be on the way to where your dreams are.

Where I stand right now with regards my dreams doesn't really matter but where I will be in ten years. The future can always be better than the present and I have the power to make it happen.

So, where are you going? Where will you be in five, ten and twenty years?
Which direction is your life going?

DAY 23

"You don't become enormously successful without encountering some really interesting problems."

Mark Victor Hansen; Author.

The bigger the challenge, the bigger the success.

Are you avoiding the big challenges coming your way in life? You are probably avoiding your big breakthroughs as well. The challenges you face and overcome today in life prepares you for tomorrow's victory.

Tackle the seemingly impossible challenges today, you will grow, you will learn and when you don't give up, you will succeed.

And oh, how happy you will be that you didn't give up. See you at the top. Keep working on your dreams, embrace the challenges, when you fail, try again and we shall definitely win.

DAY 24

"Don't limit yourself. Many people limit
themselves to what they think they can do.
You can go as far as your mind lets you. What
you believe, remember, you can achieve."

Vince Lombardi; American Football Coach.

The limitation is always in our minds. We believe we either can
or we cannot. It is always our mindset dictating what is
possible and what is not possible.

I believe that I can do all things if I will. It is a matter of your
personal conviction. We have discussed the importance of
developing a mindset of unlimited potential. Use your
imagination to go beyond your limitations.

Allow yourself to go as far as you can go. Allow yourself to do
the things you are afraid to do. Allow yourself to go beyond
what's possible or not according to the status quo.

You can be more than you think you can, allow yourself to
stretch beyond the limitations.

DAY 25

"The difference between a successful person and others is not lack of strength, not a lack of knowledge, but rather a lack of will."

Mary Kay Ash; Businesswoman & founder of Mary Kay Cosmetics.

A man or woman can do anything if he or she will. It is the will to do it which makes the difference. It is not a matter of "if you can", but "if you will?"
If you are willing then there is a way for there is always way where there is a will.

It's the decision and the commitment to get things done which underline success. We often focus on external factors and allow them to dictate what we do. Switch your focus to developing a strong will to do it. If you will, then take action and begin to see things align in your favour.

DAY 26

"Just keep going. Everybody gets better if
they keep at it."

Ted Williams; American Baseball Player.

If you have made the decision to pursue your dream, walk
right on to the end. When you don't stop, you only get better
and you will succeed.

There are so many reasons to stop, challenges, obstacles and
hurdles but all you have to do is to find one reason to keep
going.

This reason could be why you are doing it. They say if you are
persistent, you will get it, if you are consistent then you will
keep it.
Consistency will overcome resistance and bring you victory
even in the face of overwhelming opposition.

DAY 27

"The greatest of all laws is the law of progressive development. Under it, in the wide sweep of things, men grow wiser as they grow older, and societies better"

Christian Bovee; Writer.

Strive for progress not perfection. How many times have heard that? How many times have you actually reminded yourself that you don't have to be perfect but you have to keep growing?

Continuous learning is the minimum requirement for success. When we are growing progressively towards a worthy ideal, it brings us a sense of fulfilment and happiness. This is what we need to boost our confidence in order to go on and accomplish great things.

If you live a whole year and never add new skills, ideas or grow in any section of your life, you probably wasted the year.

I took some time off Facebook for the month of January this year, I spent that time to write this book, create videos for my YouTube channel and learn how to use coral draw. I got better.

What are you progressing towards? Are you going to end the year with the same skills set you had from the beginning?

DAY 28

"When you rule your mind, you rule your world"

Bill Provost; Bill Provost. Men of Integrity, Vol. 2, no. 4.

Mental fortitude is essential to keep us traveling the path to our dreams. If you are losing in your mind you can't win in life.

Don't let your environment dictate your moves, be resolute in your mind and make a conscious deliberate determined effort to never give up.

How do you rule your mind?

Be in control, be decisive, don't procrastinate. Using **the 5 seconds rule** by Mel Robbins, count 5, 4, 3, 2, and 1, and act. If you haven't read her book, I recommend it to you.

When you make a decision, act. Think through problems, come up with your own decisions and don't simply accept what is thrown at you. Soon, you will realize that you are in control of your mind. Watch less of television, don't feed on news from the media because it skews your attention and has a way of ruling your mind without you realizing you are taking an entrenched position to issues.

If you are looking to make an impact in your world, begin by taking control of your mind and what you do every day.

DAY 29

"The mind is everything; what you think, you become"

Buddha; Spiritual Teacher

Your thought literally translates into action. You are what you think about all day.

Pastor Chris in his book THE POWER OF THE MIND describes how intricate and powerful the human mind is. This organ has the ability to produce anything we feed it. You can't feed your mind with negativity and expect positive results.

One thing I want you to do today as you go out and for the rest of your life is to stand as a guard at the door of your mind.

Control everything that goes in and out of your mind. Don't allow garbage into your mental faculty. You have the power to decide what goes in and what comes out.

Don't listen to the news sometimes, if you would. Free your mind from worry and the distractions out there. Focus on becoming your best. I am not saying run away from difficulties or ignore the negatives, I am saying choose to focus on becoming your best and that means shutting out everything which distracts you from your purpose.

In the end, decide in your mind what you want and don't let anyone distract you from it.

DAY 30

"By the mind one is bound, by the mind one is freed…he who asserts with strong conviction, "I am not bound, I am free, 'becomes free"

Ramakrishna (beloved Indian mystic)

We are still talking about the power of the mind. The day I came to the stark realization that I have the power to decide what kind of life I want to live, I took the power away from society, from friends, from teachers and I became responsible for my decisions.
I owned my mind and began to live in the direction of my dreams. Most people don't even know they don't really own their minds. They don't make their own decisions.

If you feel enslaved in your mind, you are enslaved. If you are free in your mind, you are free. Mental slavery is worse than physical slavery. People who don't like to read for instance are to me are living with a small perspective of the world in their minds.

Begin today to expose your mind to the boundaries of the world. Read, stretch your mind, find new information, consume them, digest it, feed your mind and never be held back in your mind.

Believe you are winning today and forever and you will most certainly will.

DAY 31

"The greatest discovery of my generation is
that a human being can alter his life by
alternating his attitudes of mind"

William James; Philosopher.

Okay, these last few days of the month of October has been
all about the mind and making the most out of it.

Let's end with this one, if only you will change your attitude of
mind, you can change your life.

What is an attitude? One dictionary definition is: "it is a
complex mental state involving beliefs and feelings and values
and dispositions to act in certain ways".

This means that all we do, how we behave and act is
dependent on our attitude of mind. If we feel like nothing ever
works in our part of the world, then nothing will work for you.
If your belief is that you can't write or sing or act, then you
can't possibly perform any of these arts.
If a man or woman develops the "can-do" attitude and
channels his or her energy into doing what he or she dreams
of, then change will happen.
It is not a question of if it's possible, it's a question of if you
think it is possible? If you begin to change your attitude of
mind, things will start changing in your life.

NOVEMBER

We are in the 11th month of the year.

Regrets or memories?

Whatever the answer is, we still have 61 days left on the calendar to make things happen.

DAY 1

"You are never too young to lead, and you should never doubt your capacity to triumph where others have not."

Kofi Annan; A Former UN Secretary

Someone did it and failed. No one from my community ever did it. No black person has been successful at it. No white person ever made the list. This isn't going to work, no one has done it before. What makes you think you will fail because someone else failed?

Before April 1954, there was this universal belief that man was not capable of running a mile in less than 4 minutes. Roger Bannister broke the record and run a mile in less than 4 minutes running 3:58 seconds.

After that till now, over 20,000 people have run a mile in less than 4 minutes. This number includes high school students. Why is that? Because now someone has done it so everyone believes he or she can do it. We are often limited and held back not to lead or try something because no one has been successful or no one ever did it before. All you have to do is to belief in yourself and remember that everything is possible, either today, tomorrow or the next day.

So, go out there and work on your plan. You are never too young or too old and you can do it regardless of the odds. People have overcome much greater odds than what you are facing.

DAY 2

"Start by doing what's necessary; then do what's possible; and suddenly you are doing the impossible".

St. Francis of Assisi; Saint.

So, how do we begin to do what seems impossible?

St. Francis of Assisi gives us a formula. Don't look too much ahead of yourself into doing the impossible. Only begin by doing what is necessary. Begin with the basics. You are looking to become a Bestselling Author, you are looking to become an actor, an artist or a doctor, a teacher or an engineer.

Becoming an Author, begin by reading, write a paragraph, don't worry so much about publishing. Just do what is necessary which is writing if you are looking to become a bestselling author. Write every day and then now it is possible to share your write ups on a blog or newspapers. Publish them in magazines, write in columns.

Soon you can do what is impossible. Publish your first book and get it out there. You have written a good book, promote it, keep writing, keep getting better and soon you may be up for the bestselling author recognition.

Don't stress the big things, concentrate on the small things and do them well.

DAY 3

"My mission in life is not merely to survive,
but to thrive; and to do so with some passion,
some compassion, some humor, and some
style".

Maya Angelou; Poet, Singer, Memoirist, and
Civil Rights Activist.

Don't just survive, take up oxygen and die. Live. Living is more than merely existing which is what most people do. We get up, go to work, get back home. Sleep, wake up the next morning and repeat the cycle.

Live a more interesting life, help people, enjoy what you do. Do so with energy and enthusiasm. You go to work all gloomy and as if someone is pushing you to a place you don't want to go.
You keep looking at your time waiting to get out of work.

Don't be too stiff on yourself. Laugh at yourself sometimes. I don't take myself too seriously sometimes. I tell myself in the mirror: "loosen up", everything will be alright.

Go out today and live your life with some style.

DAY 4

"Life is about making an impact, not making an income".

Kevin Kruse; Professor of History, Princeton University.

All throughout the year, we have read quotes about focusing on making a difference instead of making money.

Many successful people say money isn't the motivation. It is the difference they can make in other people's lives. The money then is only a reward for helping others.

Focus on the difference you want to make, focus on the impact you want to make and not on the money. Focusing on making an income will distract you from your purpose. It has never been about the money for me. I am so focused on helping others and giving them what I have. I need money, I just don't want it but I am never driven to do something because of money. I took my first job without negotiating. I was more concerned with who I will become not what I could get.

In the end, I know the money will come only as a reward for the work I do. Impact first before income. Take that new job and don't worry so much about how much they are paying, at for the first 6 months. Go and do a job so much that the boss will ask himself or herself, if he or she is paying you enough?

DAY 5

"Strive not to be a success, but rather to be of value"

Albert Einstein; Theoretical Physicist & Nobel Prize Winner

From one of the most brilliant minds of our time. Albert Einstein shares a thought provoking message in this quote.

People pay for value. They pay for the value you bring to the market place. Don't seek success, concentrate on building yourself into a valuable person.

One that people can count on. People can call on you to do things for them and then you will get paid for it.

Don't be focused on getting there so much that you forget the journey. The process is much more important. Develop your skills, progressively enhance your craft and begin to be noticed and the world will pay attention to you.

DAY 6

"It doesn't matter if you try and try and try again, and fail. It does matter if you try and fail, and fail to try again."

Charles Kettering; Businessman & Inventor.

You are only a failure when you stop trying. Falling down is allowed but getting up is mandatory.

In a boxing match, falling down doesn't signify the end of the match, the match is ended when a boxer fails or refuses to get up after falling down.

I have watched boxing bouts where a boxer falls down but gets up and wins the match in the end.

Try and fail but don't fail to try. When you are pursuing your dreams, remember you will encounter levels of failure but don't be stopped.

Fall seven times, get up eight times. You can fail 100 times, you only need to be right once to succeed.

Go out today and keep trying. We shall win, maybe not immediately but definitely.

DAY 7

> "If you hear a voice within you say "you cannot paint," then by all means paint and that voice will be silenced."

Vincent Van Gogh; Artist.

Action trumps everything. Many are held back because they refuse to take action. We speculate, plan, draw agendas but never take action.

The only way to overcome doubt, overcome fear and give yourself the permission to shine is to take action on your dream.

Action banishes fear and doubt. When you begin, it carries so much power and you are much more likely to finish what you started than to finish what you never started.

So, do it. Paint, write, sing, act, play, and win.

DAY 8

"There is only one way to avoid criticism: do nothing, say nothing, and be nothing."

Aristotle; Philosopher.

This is the quote you should never forget. Never allow what people will say to determine what you do with your life. People are going to judge you regardless, so why don't you give them something to judge.

People will talk anyway so why bother about what they will say? Give them something to talk about. Live your life, do something great. As long as you are not progressing or doing something worthwhile in life, you are free from criticism. No one will bother talking about you or vilify you.

You will be misunderstood, laughed at, scorned, embarrassed, criticized when you decide to stand out of the crowd especially when you succeed.
You know why? Because your success robs them of their excuse for failure. If we all fail, then I can say everyone failed. But if you go out there and win, then you deny them their excuse for failure.

If you can get to a point in your life where the opinions of men don't matter anymore, you are ready to do great things.

DAY 9

"Ask and it will be given to you; search, and
you will find; knock and the door will be
opened for you."

Jesus Christ of Nazareth

If you don't ask, the answer is always no. What you seek you
get. This biblical principle transcends Christianity.

In the world we live, those who are not afraid of asking always
get what they need. Most of us never ask because we feel we
don't want to appear weak. Asking doesn't make you weak, it
only means you want to remain strong.

What do you need? Ask. Knock on the door and believe that
you will find what you seek.

The universe has a way of giving back what we put out there.
When we believe that God will answer our prayers, He will.

You don't have answers yet because you don't ask. You
haven't found what you are looking for because you are not
really seeking it.
Don't be afraid to ask because when you don't ask, the answer
is always no.

DAY 10

---

*"I think of doing a series as very hard work.
But then I've talked to coal miners, and that's
really hard work."*

William Shatner; Actor.

I had an experience like that when I was in college. I got home for one vacation and went out to help a group of workers building a temple.

I was going to help them carry bricks to the building site.

After the fourth trip, I was broken. I couldn't believe these guys have been working under the hot sun all day and they are still going while I am panting.

That was when I knew I had to make use of my mental power and never my physical power. That is why I read every day. I learn every day because I need to exercise my mind to be able to exert my mental power.

So, don't complain, your work may be hard but I know a group of fishermen in my community who work themselves to death.

DAY 11

"Definiteness of purpose is the starting point
of all achievement.

W. Clement Stone; Businessman.

Do you really know for sure what you want in life? How clear are you on your vision or purpose?

Sometimes we say we want to lose weight but we are only pretending we want to lose weight. How much weight are we willing to lose?

Watch how you behave when you are around potato chips or bread with peanut butter. Can we resist not taking a bite of a burger?

To begin the journey to your dream, you need to be able to define exactly what you want and why you want it. With these clearly defined, you are well equipped to go through the process of getting there.

Don't dilly dally about it, be definite in your decision making.

Today, write down what you really want and why you want it. Then you can start.

DAY 12

"Life isn't about getting and having, it's about giving and being."

Kevin Kruse; Professor of History, Princeton University

Nothing in nature was made for itself. A tree doesn't produce oxygen for its own consumption, human beings don't use carbon dioxide for ourselves. A tree doesn't produce fruits for itself. Imagine if trees held on to oxygen and human beings held on to carbon dioxide. What would happen?

Human beings will die and the trees would also die. There is a saying, "when the last tree dies, the last man dies".

Life is really about giving and being. You think you would be better off when everyone dies and you are left with the wealth of the world? Who would cook, mow your grass, attend to you when you are sick, build, paint, sing; we as human beings can only enjoy the life we live when we give of what we have. That is when we feel our being.

If you are always looking to get, accumulate and hoard, you are not going to live a fulfilled life. Give of your time, your loyalty, your love, your money, your talent and see how you come alive as others also give to you. This is not only a Biblical principle but a principle which works even in contemporary world.

DAY 13

"The most common way people give up their
power is by thinking they don't have any."

Alice Walker; Novelist.

We all have our superpowers. There is something we can do
well and that gives us our power.

When we are oblivious to the fact that we all have something
we are good at, something that if we are not around to do
can't be done as well as when we are around, we don't really
see our importance.

Don't let what others do or can do make you feel powerless.
Don't relinquish your power, hold on to what you are good at
even if it's a handful of sand. Develop it, that's your leverage
in life.

Find your power and don't give it up. There is power in you.

DAY 14

"The best time to plant a tree was 20 years ago. The second-best time is now."

Chinese Proverb

I included this Chinese proverb not only for the planting of trees but also to tell you that there is nothing like it's too late to do what you should have done twenty years ago.

You should have written a book twenty years ago, you can still write it today. You should have started the business five years ago, now others are running a similar business idea, you think it's too late for you, no, you can still do it. No one can do it the way you wanted to do it.

Life offers us second chances sometimes but we look back so much on the past that instead of taking advantage of the present opportunity, we don't. We rather spend our time regretting what we should have and could have done.

20 years later, you are alive, you can plant that tree today, you can plant that idea today. Are you going to sit around and regret another twenty years to come what you are failing to do today?

DAY 15

"Eighty percent of success is showing up."

Woody Allen; Filmmaker

Imagine a student refusing to go to the exams room because he or she doesn't feel ready to take the exams. Saying, I am not well prepared and I am probably going to fail.

Yes, you are probably going to fail because you are refusing to show up.

Have you seen the questions and how do you know you can't answer them?

Take today's advice to heart, always show up even when you are not prepared. When you show up, you have the opportunity to win, if you don't, you already lost.

You have a meeting, show up. Be there, contribute, you never know when your big break will come.

DAY 16

"Winning isn't everything, but wanting to win
is."

Vince Lombardi; American Football Coach.

It is the desire which gives birth to the result. When you get into the game, go with the winning mentality.

Remember, when you are losing in your mind, you can't win in life. You have to be determined in your mind to succeed. That determination gives you a competitive edge.

It is not so much about winning but the desire to win. The decision to give it your best. That is the drive, the passion that will lead to winning.

Whatever project you are working on, the success of it begins with the desire to succeed at it.

DAY 17

"I am not a product of my circumstances. I am a product of my decisions."

Stephen Covey; Author & Businessman.

It is true that some people find themselves in an environment which makes it easy and possible to thrive and succeed.

Others find themselves in situations or circumstances which make succeeding difficult. Born to poor parents, raised in a poor village, had no access to basic education, living in a violent community, all of these circumstances are real and undeniably huge obstacles to succeeding in life.

The truth is, nothing has the power to stop you from becoming your dream. Our decision, our choices define us more than our circumstances.

As George Barnard Shaw said, "those who succeed look out for the circumstances they need to succeed and if they don't find them, they create them".

Never succumb to your environment, never allow the story of your birth, the community you grew up in or what happened in your past to stop you from living your purpose.

It's your life now and your decisions will determine who you become now. Decide.

DAY 18

"You can never cross the ocean until you have
the courage to lose sight of the shore."

Christopher Columbus; Explorer & Colonizer.

Safety net. Some people are always looking for safety nets before they take any risk. There are people who think they are taking a leap of faith but all they are doing is trying not to jump too high and having a safety net, just in case they fall.

If you keep looking back then you will run back when things get tough. When I begin any project or a new book, I close the door behind me.

When there is no way back, it will amaze you how you can come up with ideas and breakthrough solutions to the problems you encounter.

It takes courage and fortitude to look on ahead and fight on. There are easy roads, there are shortcuts and escape routes on the way to the dream and you need the courage to ignore all of them, so you don't settle for less than you dream of.

If you are looking to do the impossible, stop holding on to your safety nets, stop being afraid of giving 100% of yourself to the dream.

We can't get to where we dream of if we are not willing to leave where we are. As we step out today, let's leave the known and venture into the unknown with the courage and faith that we will get to our destination.

DAY 19

"Conditions are never perfect. 'Someday' is a disease that will take your dreams to the grave with you.... If it's important to you and you want to do it 'eventually,' just do it and correct course along the way."

Tim Ferriss; Author & Public Speaker.

We often get caught up with preparing and analyzing every single detail we over-prepare and over-analyze. We become too cautious and this stops us from ever going forward.

I believe we should always be doing either of one of these two things in our lives. One, we have to discover what we really want to do, what our purpose on earth is, what we are passionate about and then, two, going out there to make sure we work on that passion, that goal, that purpose till we succeed.

Most people spend all their time on the first one, trying to figure out what is it they are here for and they never get to the second part which is actually doing something, however small about it. Taking action on your dream is everything. Without action, nothing will work.

You are passionate about your dream but passion is an emotion without an action. Passion wouldn't make your dreams come true unless you act on your passion. You have to take a step to get what you want. We all need passion and inner drive in order to succeed.

Just don't keep the passion and inner drive inside. Put them into action.

What we are talking about here is **progress not perfection**. The reason most people never get started, never take action is because they want to be great from the beginning but no one starts being great. You have to start to become great.

DAY 20

"The two most important days in your life are the day you are born and the day you find out why."

Mark Twain; Writer, Humourist & Lecturer

Yesterday, I talked about the two primary choices we have in life. I said, I believe we should always be doing either of one of these two things in our lives. One, we have to discover what we really want to do, what our purpose on earth is, what we are passionate about and then, two, going out there to make sure we work on that passion, that goal, that purpose till we succeed.

The day you were born was the first important day in your life, discovering why you were born and pursuing that purpose is the next important thing. Many are born but spend most of their lives without ever coming to the knowledge of why they were born. Some people find their purpose at an early age, others in their mid-age, while others in their old age.

The worst of it all are those who give up on finding their purpose. They simply drift through life without anyone ever knowing they were here. If you have found your purpose, live it, you don't need anyone's permission. If you haven't found it yet, keep looking.

DAY 21

"Whatever you can do, or dream you can,
begin it. Boldness has genius, power and
magic in it."

Johann Wolfgang von Goethe; Writer &
German Stateman.

There is a great power which comes with starting or beginning a project. Just start and I know some people will ask, how do you start? First, write down what you want to get done. Write a book, paint your room, arrange your books on the shelves, you have an essay to finish or you have to analyze data for your boss. You will be tempted to look at the enormity of the task and postpone it. If I have to write a 10-page essay for school. I may be tempted to say, "when am I going to finish?" Then, I will give up entirely.

So, one way to become productive and get it done is to **simply start**. Don't worry about how long it will take you to finish. When I wanted to write my first book, there were lots of things I didn't know and that could have deterred me but I just started and the rest they say is history. There is power in starting. Stop talking and start.

Another reason why starting will make you productive is because of what is called **ZEIGARNIK EFFECT**. In **psychology, the Zeigarnik effect states that people remember uncompleted or interrupted tasks better than completed tasks.**

There is a sense of unfulfillment. Due to this effect, we are likely to go on to finish once we have the courage to start. Don't wait to feel like doing it before you start. Once you know what you want to do, count 1 to 5 and then just start.

DAY 22

> "People often say that motivation doesn't last. Well, neither does bathing. That's why we recommend it daily."

Zig Ziglar; Author, Salesman and Motivational Speaker.

Motivation or discipline? When motivation ends, discipline takes over.

Motivation doesn't last, that's true. There are days extrinsic motivation wouldn't get you out of bed. What you need is discipline. A mix of motivation and discipline will get you to your destination.

There is something peculiar about motivation, it is like lighting a fire, it can burn very hot but you know it is surely going to die down. You have to light another fire.

That's motivation. It burns like fire and if you don't use it, if you don't get up and do something with it, it dies down.

So, you always need to light another fire. I like the way Zig puts it, "we recommend it every day".

I listen to motivational tapes every morning when I wake up, it could be a podcast on personal development or a sermon. I make sure I listen for 30 to 45 minutes.

As you won't forget to take your bath today, don't forget to fire up your mind with some motivation for the day.

DAY 23

"Life shrinks or expands in proportion to one's courage."

Anais Nin; Essayist.

To dare is to rise above challenges and it takes courage. The more you dare, the more courageous you can be, the more your life expands as to how much you can accomplish.

If you are always holding on and never letting yourself take action on your dream, you will be in the same place.

Courage doesn't mean the absence of fear or doubt, courage is saying to yourself even though I might fail I am still going to do it.

Many people have the talent and the desire to succeed but they don't have the gut to fail. It takes courage to say regardless of the odds, I will do it.

If you are not making some mistakes, you haven't been very courageous because you have been playing safe. If you are looking to live your life fulfilling your purpose, begin by feeling the fear and doing it anyway. This is how you will develop the courage to keep confronting your fears and doubt, soon your confidence will grow.

DAY 24

"The only person you are destined to become
is the person you decide to be."

Ralph Waldo Emerson; Essayist, Lecturer &
Philosopher.

We don't succeed in life by destiny, we succeed in life by determination. You can only go as far as you can see, your vision determines who you become.

If you don't have a vision then you have no idea who you are even becoming. Every man or woman has the power to become whoever or whatever he or she wants to become but it begins with the clear vision of that person.

Where do you see yourself in five or ten years? Where do you see yourself in twenty years? Have that vision of yourself, hold that vision in your mind and begin to work towards it, as you go through the day, whatever you are doing, ask yourself, is what I am doing helping me to become the person I see in my mind?

Decide who you want to be and don't let anyone talk you out of it.

DAY 25

"Go confidently in the direction of your dreams. Live the life you have imagined."

Henry David Thoreau; Essayist, Poet & Philosopher

Yesterday I talked about having a clear vision and holding it in your mind. It takes confidence to work towards what you see in your mind especially when others around you can't see it. It requires confidence in yourself when others are doubting you, and when you are doubting yourself if you can become that person you are seeing yourself to be.

Once you hold that image in your mind, don't let go of it, begin the journey in the direction of that dream. Like I said yesterday, whatever you do should align with becoming that person.

Use that vision as the yardstick to measure everything you do. Let it be your litmus test to test everything you do, if it is not contributing to you becoming that person, then avoid it.

If there are people in your life who are not helping you go in the direction of your dream, don't take them along.

I am not saying don't be friends with them just don't tell them anything as they will be of no help to your journey. Sometimes, it's okay to leave some people behind.

You can help them after you have done it. Let's stay on the path and never lose the vision in our minds. If we don't give up, we will become what we dream of.

DAY 26

"When I stand before God at the end of my life, I would hope that I would not have a single bit of talent left and could say, I used everything you gave me."

Erma Bombeck; Humourist.

This is my prayer too and I hope it is yours as well.

At the end of our lives, the most important question will be, "who did you become and how many lives were better because you were here?"

Someone said, "our life is God's gift to us and what we do with it is our gift back to God".

What gift are you giving back to God? You don't have to do big things, not everyone will be out there doing things on a large scale.
However small, we can all make an impact, draw, paint, write, speak to little children, sing, dance, play the violin, whatever you do, do it to the best of your ability.

Give it your all, and then give some more. Let someone's life be better because you were here.

We all have our talents, and it doesn't have to be shiny and huge, it only has to be useful even in small ways.
My books may not be translated into a thousand languages but if I can help a thousand people live a better life, I think that will count for something.

Ask yourself every day, am I using it all up or is there more I can do?

DAY 27

"Few things can help an individual more than
to place responsibility on him, and to let him
know that you trust him."

Booker T. Washington; Educator, Orator &
Author.

Do this for yourself and not just people. The moment you
accept responsibility for your life, you feel in charge of
yourself.
Human beings they say are animals of necessity. When we
have to build a house in a thick forest in order to survive, we
will build that house with our bare hands.

If we are to build a boat so we can get off the island, we are
going to build that boat whether we have the tools or not. It is
in our nature to come up with solutions when it is a matter of
life and death, when it becomes necessary.

When we sense no real danger, or have no need to do
something, we relax, we joke around. It's the same when you
give someone responsibility for something or you make
yourself responsible for something, immediately you do that,
there is a sense of duty and necessity.

If you can trust yourself to finish the project you have started, you are going to complete it successfully. Giving people responsibility gives them a sense of important and trust.

DAY 28

"Certain things catch your eye, but pursue
only those that capture the heart."

Ancient Indian Proverb

What we don't see is a lot more complex than what we see.

Our physical eyes can only see as far as it can see, what our souls are really searching for cannot be seen with our eyes but with our hearts.

Don't go chasing what only the eyes can see, pursue the things you desire in your heart even when you have no physical evidence of it happening. Hold on to what captures your heart.

That is why I believe in mind sight more than eye sight. Lots of things will capture your eyes, don't be distracted, pursue the things which bring meaning to your life.

DAY 29

"Everything you've ever wanted is on the other side of fear."

George Addair; Real Estate Developer.

It takes courage to cross to the other side. It takes courage to publish a book. It takes courage to start a family. It takes courage to start a business. To go to college. It takes courage to outdoor your painting. It takes courage to say I will go back to college and finish my degree.

Fear is very destructive, it can hold us captive and never allow us to reach our dreams. If only we can develop the courage to overcome our fear, our dreamland will soon become reality land. Identify what makes you afraid; that you will lose, that you will be ridiculed, make sure you can define what really makes you afraid and then eliminate it.

Once you can identify what you are really afraid of or what fuels your fear, you have taken a big step towards overcoming it. You can't overcome what you don't know. So, find out what is really making you afraid because sometimes we don't even know. I thought my fear was I was too young to write my first book but my real fear was I felt I wasn't good enough and people would laugh at me. Once I knew that, I knew how to deal with it. I got to the other side of my fear.

DAY 30

"Luck? I don't know anything about luck. I've never banked on it, and I'm afraid of people who do. Luck to me is something else: hard work -- and realizing what is opportunity and what isn't."

Lucille Ball; Actress, Comedian and Model.

I once had a little debate on Facebook with one young man who didn't agree with me that there is no such thing as luck. I knew some would not agree with me here too but I will make my point. I am still open to learning.

Our definition of luck is that someone got something he or she didn't work hard for or deserved, or something happened by chance or someone succeeded at something just because of some divine fate.

To me, luck is when opportunity meets preparation. Hard work puts you in a better position to be "lucky". Like I said, no one succeeds by destiny but by determination.

There is no such thing as luck, often, as someone once said, luck is a word we use to describe the success of people we don't like.

Work hard and create your own opportunity, which some people call luck.

DECEMBER

We are in the 12th month of the year.

I am glad we made this journey together. We are grateful for the gift of life.

However, the year has been, it has been of lessons and success. For the times when we went through tough situations, we still made it through.

The year is not over yet, we still have 31 days left. We can still make the rest of the year the best of the year.

Believe!

DAY 1

"We can easily forgive a child who is afraid of the dark;
the real tragedy of life is when men are afraid of the
light."

Plato; Philosopher.

We don't want to be exposed. We are afraid to put our stuff out there for fear of being criticized, for fear of being ridiculed. We take the backseat even in our own lives. We are afraid to talk, we are afraid to stand up because we are afraid of the light.

We rather hide in the darkness. We rather not speak up, we are afraid we will be criticized. If a child is hiding, we can excuse him or her but if a man or woman is afraid to come out and do what he or she knows they should be doing, that is a real tragedy. I was at a point afraid the light will expose my inadequacies, my weakness, my frailties but who doesn't have them?

I couldn't possibly do anything about them until I exposed them to the light. I put my writings out there, got criticized, got better, got corrected, got better, kept writing, now I am standing in the light.

You are bad at playing the piano? Come out and get some help. Stop hiding in the dark.

DAY 2

"Teach thy tongue to say, "I do not know," and thou shalt progress."

Maimonides; Philosopher.

Asking questions, something which took me a long time to come to grips with it.

I always thought I was too smart to figure everything out on my own. I never wanted to appear weak by saying "I don't know".

I am smart, I am intelligent, so why should say "I don't know"?

I would always figure it out on my own. It may take me days or weeks but I will still find out.

What I didn't know was that I could have simply learned in a minute from someone who had the answer if I simply learned how to say I don't know, please "teach" me.

I would have progressed faster in life and I have been progressing ever since I learned this profound truth.

Learn to teach your tongue to say, "I don't know" and you will only be wiser to learn from other people and move faster in life.

DAY 3

"When I was 5 years old, my mother always told me that happiness was the key to life. When I went to school, they asked me what I wanted to be when I grew up. I wrote down 'happy'. They told me I didn't understand the assignment, and I told them they didn't understand life."

John Lennon; Singer-Songwriter.

If we can use this as the measuring tool for everything we do in life, we will be happy 90% of the time.

Is the book I am writing now going to make me happy ten years from now? Will I be happy with this job I am taking? Will I be happy with the person I am with?

Happiness is the yardstick, if it is not making you happy, then it is probably going to kill you. It is not only about your profession or what you do. It is not where you come from, it is not how much money you have, it is about your decision to be happy.

Happiness is an inside job. There is no key to happiness, the door is always open.

DAY 4

"Everything has beauty, but not everyone can see."

Confucius; Philosopher.

Many people look but cannot see. Seeing is a thing of the mind, looking is a function of the eye.

Seeing is when you bring meaning or interpretation to what you are looking at. Even in our troubles, even in our challenges, if we can see the reason behind why we had to endure these challenges, we shall see the beauty in it.

The people we associate with may not be what we want them to be, their physical beauty, their character, etc. but if we can look well enough, we shall see their beauty.

Look beyond their weaknesses, their physical inadequacies and you shall see the beauty beyond the eyes. When we judge people, we fail to see their beauty. Everyone has something beautiful, be conscious about seeing it. Don't always dwell on the negative.

DAY 5

"How wonderful it is that nobody need wait a single moment before starting to improve the world."

Anne Frank; Diarist.

Really, you don't need anyone's permission to pursue your dreams. All you need is your own belief and determination to change your life and to make an impact in the world.

You don't have to wait for anyone or anything. If you have an idea, a dream and you believe in it, go out there and work on it.

I realized there were lots of quote books out there but I wanted to improve on it. So, I wrote this one. I believe in these quotes and I live by them that is why I am so passionate about sharing them with my thoughts.

If you have been thinking of something, go out there and do it.

DAY 6

"When I let go of what I am, I become what I might be."

Lao Tzu; Philosopher

We are all at a stage in our lives now, where we could be more than we are now if we have the courage to let go off what we are now.

It takes massive determination and belief to leave the shores of our current life in search of what we can become.
Every human being carries potential and just like potential energy, it is only by virtue of its position.

In order to make use of this potential, we have to put it into work, into motion and turn it into kinetic energy.

If you are willing to put your potential energy to work, you shall move from where you are to where you can be.

Don't stay here, you are made for more. Let's move.

DAY 7

"Life is not measured by the number of breaths we take, but by the moments that take our breath away."

Maya Angelou; Poet, Singer, Memoirist, and Civil Rights Activist.

Memories not regrets. Life should be about making memories. Be involved in things you love to do, help people and make other people's lives meaningful because you are here.

Every day we go out, we should be thinking more about what I can do today so I can look back tomorrow and smile.

Every day may not go as planned, but we should strive to make it better. What we do for others brings us joy, how we make other people feel is something they will remember for the rest of their lives.

Don't worry about how long you will be on earth, how many breaths you will take, work on things that are meaningful to you and humanity.

DAY 8

"Happiness is not something readymade. It comes from
your own actions."

Dalai Lama; Monk of the Gelug School.

Remember, there is no key to happiness, the door is always
open. Don't expect other people to make you happy, it's too
much of a job to give to others, you will be disappointed most
of the time.

Happiness is not for sale. You have to manufacture it. You
have to find the right ingredients, find the things you are
passionate about and do them. Do what you have to do with
love and see how happiness builds up in your heart.

Every action you take should lead to your happiness, don't
react to what people do to you or against you. It doesn't
matter what someone else said or did to you, you can always
choose to be happy instead of being bitter or sad.

Remember, you are in control of your happiness, your actions
and reactions determine your happiness.

DAY 9

"If you're offered a seat on a rocket ship, don't ask what seat! Just get on."

Sheryl Sandberg; <u>Chief Operating Officer of Facebook</u>

Some opportunities are to be taken without looking for comfort or asking lots of questions. If it is something you have been preparing or waiting for, then when the opportunity presents itself, jump on and find your bearings later as you journey on. I told you earlier in the book that one of my goals this year was to write movie scripts. I had a friend contact me about writing scripts for short movies, I had just started reading online and watching tutorials on YouTube on how to write scripts but I said yes.

He asked when I could submit my first script so his team can look at it. I gave him a date which was a week away. I quickly went online and spent hours learning on writing scripts. I got to work and on the night of the day I promised to send the script, I did send the script. The next morning, I got a message from him saying, "the script is great, how long have you been doing this?"
So, no hesitation, jump on and figure it out later. Some opportunities never come back. Jump and grow your wings down.

DAY 10

"First, have a definite, clear practical ideal; a goal, an objective. Second, have the necessary means to achieve your ends; wisdom, money, materials, and methods. Third, adjust all your means to that end."

Aristotle; Philosopher.

This is a good recipe for becoming successful. All summed in a single quote, this is why I love reading and applying quotes in my life. A year ago, I decided to put together my own quote book. And I didn't want it to be just like any other quote book. I wanted it to be different.

My definite clear practical ideal was a quote book with a few paragraphs of exposition I could read before I start my day every day of the year. The goal therefore was to collect my best 365 quotes out of the thousands of quotes I have read.

The necessary means in this example was the collection of quotes, the ability to write and relate them to everyday life, I had the wisdom to apply what I know, the materials and the method to publish it on Amazon and the money I invested into a cover design and formatting.

The third part was to adjust everything until this book became successful.

I have applied this formula in my daily life and have always come up successful. Sometimes challenges show up along the way but with persistence you will always get there.

DAY 11

"If the wind will not serve, take to the oars."

Latin Proverb

There is always a way out of the challenge. Don't rely on the norm to get things done. We need the wind to move but if you reach a point in life where the help you need, the people you count on and the opportunities you seek don't come as expected, use other means necessary to get to the goal. Take to the oars.

Get to work, use the paddles. Start paddling away. Winners always find a way to win when it seems they are losing.

People who blame the wind will never win. You may have to work twice as hard but whatever it takes don't give up, when the wind isn't serving you, take the oars.

We will get there by one way or the other but we will still get there.

DAY 12

"You can't fall if you don't climb. But there's no joy in living your whole life on the ground."

Unknown

There is a South African proverb which says; **"Not everyone who chased the zebra caught it, but the one who caught the zebra chased it."**

Profound, right? Yeah. I love this, absolutely. Running after the zebra doesn't give you a guarantee that you will catch it but if you don't run after the zebra then there is no guarantee at all. If you take the action and chase it, then there is a probability however small that you may catch it.

Now, consider the one who never chased the zebra. There is no chance, not even 0.00001% chance of ever catching the zebra. Some say, well, then you will never be disappointed in life. If you don't try, you can't lose and you won't be disappointed.

Many are held back by the fear of losing and never venture into anything with the slightest risk. Afraid of making mistakes, afraid of being embarrassed, afraid of losing, afraid of not catching the zebra.

You can decide not to run after the zebra because you may not catch it or you can decide to go after it because you may catch it. It is safe to not run after the zebra which is what a lot of people choose to do. Keep thinking and strategizing but never go out there to chase the zebra. They have a map for chasing zebras. They have a plan for chasing zebras. They have ideas about chasing zebras but they have never chased any zebras in their life.

They have ideas about climbing mountains, they are strategizing on how not to fall. They don't have a good plan yet as they keep analyzing so much that they have never even tried it.

If you don't jump, you won't fall but what is the use of your life if you spend all your time on the ground? Then why did you even come here?

Why choose to be a spectator when you can be on the field?

DAY 13

"We must believe that we are gifted for something, and that this thing, at whatever cost, must be attained."

Marie Curie; Physicist.

It is with this belief that we attain great feats. If you don't believe you are here for something special, then you will live an ordinary life.

We should always believe we are made for more. We should never be distracted by our surroundings or circumstances, we should always be striving for a place beyond yonder.

It is necessary to commit to making your dream possible. Dreams never give up on us but we do give up on our dreams. When we do come to the realization that we are here for something much more than to live and die, we will make every effort to live our purpose.

You are gifted for something great, live it!

DAY 14

"A life without challenges is a boring one"

Aliko Dangote; Businessman & African Richest man.

Coming from the richest man in Africa, he has had his fair share of challenges in his business life. He stated this in an interview I was watching where he was sharing his advice on what it takes to build success.

The challenges we face in life are designed to take us to the next level and if we are always looking to avoid challenges then we are looking to avoid our promotion.

Let me add this one from Joshua J. Marine: "Challenges are what make life interesting and overcoming them is what makes life meaningful."

So, embrace your challenges, don't live a boring life. I believe that challenges come to those who have the seed of the solutions in them, challenges gravitate towards those who have their solutions.

When you begin to experience challenges in your life, remind yourself, these challenges are coming to me because I have the solution in me.

DAY 15

"If you want to lift yourself up, lift up someone else."

Booker T. Washington; Educator, Orator & Author.

This sums up the essence of life. No one ever became great just by making other people smaller. You don't become big by shrinking other people.

When you live your life to make others life better, you are fulfilling a divine principle which makes it possible for you to lift yourself.
Every help you give others is recorded somehow by the universe and you will get your reward. "You reap what you sow", the Bible says. Often, we look at the negative aspect of this quote but we should focus on the positive aspect.

The investment we make in other peoples' lives will find a way to come back to us. I believe this.

If you are looking to become great or lift yourself up, think of how you can make other people come up as well. Think of how you can make other people's lives better.

Selfishness and me-first won't make you go higher. I am not talking about not taking care of yourself, take care of yourself, you can't pour from an empty cup but always be looking out for who you can pour in, when you give you create vacuum to receive.

If you are holding on to what you have then you can never be filled with new and better things. Empty yourself, make room so you can be filled with more.

DAY 16

"I have been impressed with the urgency of doing. Knowing is not enough; we must apply. Being willing is not enough; we must do."

Leonardo da Vinci; Painter, Sculptor, Engineer, Architect & Scientist

---

There is a gap between knowledge and wisdom. Knowledge is just information and as I shared in my book **31 DAYS OF WISDOM**, when we don't apply what we know, it serves no purpose. Contrary to popular belief, knowledge isn't power, applied knowledge is power.

Just having a bunch of ideas and information without really doing anything doesn't give you power. It is when we take action with what we know then things begin to change. Of course, if you just want to sit at one place and expect things to change, they never will. Wisdom is the application of knowledge.

There is always a price to pay for success and more so there is a price to pay when you want things your way. For instance, if you know that you have to stop watching movies or television for a while in order to get something, and then you have no other option but shut down the computer and switch off the television. I had to sacrifice some sleep, some going out time and some movie time to finish this book. Most people often end up being their own enemies. They act in a way that hinders them from succeeding. Self-sabotaging their dreams by not taking action on them. Giving into small indulgences like watching music videos instead of studying.

If all we do is to have knowledge and not apply, be willing and never do anything, then we are getting nowhere. Apply what you know and just don't be willing but actually go out there and take action on your dreams.

DAY 17

"Limitations live only in our minds. But if we use our imaginations, our possibilities become limitless."

Jamie Paolinetti; Film Actor.

I first heard Roger Federal use this quote in an interview and I quickly wrote it down. It gives me a lot of meaning.

We can choose to expand the borders of our limitations if we can expand it in our minds.

The things you think you can or cannot do is all in your mind. The day you decide you are going to go beyond what's impossible, these limitations expand and allow your new mindset and believe to explore the possibilities of what you can do.

Imagine great things, imagine your success, ignore your limitations, ignore the obstacles, focus on how far you can go and you can go far.

Don't allow the things you see around you to dictate how far you can go in life. You only have to allow your mind to see beyond what your eyes can see. If you allow your imagination to begin to see beyond what's possible or not, you will be in a state of unlimited possibilities.

DAY 18

"You take your life in your own hands, and what happens? A terrible thing, no one to blame."

Erica Jong; Novelist.

Don't we all love to blame others for our inadequacies? Isn't it easier to complain about things than to fix them?

Isn't it easy to find fault than to find remedy?

For those looking to succeed, taking responsibility of their life is not a bargain. It is something they embrace with enthusiasm.

They don't blame their parents, the government or the society, there are no scapegoats and your friends have no part to share in the blame game. You simply take responsibility for your life.

You look yourself in the mirror and say to yourself, from today, I am going to be responsible for myself and whether I will succeed or not, it is my responsibility and I am going to make it happen.

This is the beginning of attaining personal success. No one is coming to save you, no amount of blame will make you successful, so, decide to be in total control of your life and begin to experience total freedom and gravitate towards the success you seek.

DAY 19

"What's success? A man is a success if he gets up in the morning and goes to bed at night and in between does what he wants to do."

Bob Dylan; Singer-Songwriter.

I believe you are having a great year. Success has been misunderstood and misinterpreted because people associate it with having a lot of money in the bank, living in a big house and driving big cars.

These things are material things. They don't define success; a successful person can own them all but that is not what makes one successful.

It is the fulfilment of doing what you love to do, spend time with people you love, helping other people and being happy.

A school teacher who loves to teach young kids, a mechanic who loves fixing cars, a singer who loves to sing, if someone loves to write, and at the end of the day you can look yourself in the mirror and be proud of what you have done then you were successful.

It is not the car you drive, the house you live in or the money you have. It is about how meaningful your life is, not just to yourself but to others.

DAY 20

> **"I didn't fail the test. I just found 100 ways to do it wrong."**

Benjamin Franklin; Founding Father of the United States.

Failure has no meaning until we give it one. How we interpret our failures determine the lessons we can learn from them.

The lessons we choose to learn from our failures determine how we make the best out of it. So, when you fail or make a mistake, look for the lessons.

Failure is not the end, it's only a detour on the road to the destination. You failed? You might as well learn your lessons, you already paid for the tuition.

You didn't fail, you just found out how not to do it. Try again and do it better this time.

DAY 21

"In order to succeed, your desire for success should be greater than your fear of failure."

Bill Cosby; Comedian.

Desire is the starting point. When you have great desire to become successful then it will trump your fears.
When your desire to succeed isn't stronger than your fears, then you will give up.
We have read that "everything you want is on the other side of your fear." It is with our desires that we can overcome this fear.

When we want something bad enough it doesn't matter what is standing between us and what we want, we will find a way around or through it.

Fear of failure stops a lot of people from attempting anything in life. Failure isn't fatal and never the end. Don't beat yourself up, rather, look on the bright side, don't focus on failing, focus on winning and you will mostly certainly will. Even when you fail, you should quickly learn your lessons and get on with your life.

Is your desire bigger than your fears?

DAY 22

"When money is seen as the solution to every problem, money itself becomes the problem"

Richard Needham; Politician.

I will share this principle of mine with you.

The same way we earn money, we can earn trust. We can earn loyalty and build relationships which will bring us great social capital. We can buy and sell with character, truth, trust, honesty, loyalty and integrity even without money. Mostly, what these values can buy money cannot buy.

In marketing and promoting my first book BECOMING YOUR DREAM and putting myself out there as a motivational speaker and an author, I earned the trust and respect of my good friend and partner, Solomon Ewusie, who did a lot of things to advance the goal without any money.

If I had money, I would have paid a well-established media firm to do the work but I would need money. Without money, I earned trust and respect which got the work done. Don't focus so much on earning money now, there are much more important things to earn.

There are a lot of millionaires who are owing bank credits and huge loans from the banks. They have earned trust, respect, integrity. When they get to the bank, because they have earned the trust and respect, the banks are not afraid to loan them money for their projects. Will come back to that.

Personally, I have done a lot of things which required money by not using money but by simply picking up the phone and calling friends who trust me, people whose respect, loyalty and trust I have earned and get things done. I have the trust of my friend, he sees I am diligent about a particular project I am working on, I don't have to let money be a source of worry, I have to work on myself, start the project and get my friend to support me.

We won't always get the support of all of our friends but we will get the support of trusted friends. So back to my point, before you worry yourself about money, earn trust, earn loyalty, build character. If your friends know you to be a fraudster, someone who doesn't pay back loans, no one will help you.

You don't always need your own money to get things done. That is one difference between the rich and the poor. Most people think they need money to do everything so they never get anything done

DAY 23

"To freely bloom - that is my definition of success"

Gerry Spence; Lawyer & Author.

What does it mean to bloom? To bloom is to bear flowers organically. A flower blooms unceasingly and it doesn't need permission to do that.
To bloom is to thrive where you are planted. It doesn't matter where you are, decide to do what you love and do it joyously.

Success therefore is the progressive realization of this purpose, to reach the point where your life is about being happy and spreading joy and making an impact in other people's lives.

Don't be stifled by life, don't allow your environment to push you down, bloom where you are planted.

DAY 24

"There are no traffic jams along the extra mile."

Roger Staubach; American Football Quarterback.

The difference between the ordinary and the extraordinary has always been the little extra. If you are looking to live the life you dream of then you have to be willing to do today what others won't do just so you can enjoy tomorrow what others won't get.

The extra mile is free because very few are willing to put in the work to get there. We all love to crowd on the common road. Someone once said, "it's lonely at the top but you eat better".

It's not easy to wake up every morning and keep working on a dream you alone can see. It's frustrating to keep investing, working and spending late nights and early mornings when others are having a good time.

If you are looking to get unto the extra mile and enjoy the ride, then be willing to put in the work now. It doesn't happen overnight.

DAY 25

"And will you succeed? Yes indeed, yes indeed! Ninety-eight and three-quarters percent guaranteed!"

Dr. Seuss; Author, Poet & Publisher.

We are often skeptical about our dreams. Is this going to work? Will it be successful? We are often held back because we are worried about what will go wrong instead of focusing on what could go right.

What if I fail? What if I make mistakes? What if I don't make it?

Oh dear! What if you succeed?

Are you worried about how this is all going to turn out? It begins with the belief that everything will work out. All you have to do is to keep working. Don't give up, believe in yourself and in your dream.

And just in case you are still worried about whether you will succeed or not? Listen to Dr. Seuss again, "Yes indeed, yes indeed! Ninety-eight and three-quarters percent guaranteed!"

We shall win, maybe not immediately but definitely.

DAY 26

"People tend to be generous when sharing their nonsense, fear, and ignorance. And while they seem quite eager to feed you their negativity, please remember that sometimes the diet we need to be on is a spiritual and emotional one. Be cautious with what you feed your mind and soul. Fuel yourself with positivity and let that fuel propel you into positive action."

Steve Maraboli; Unapologetically You: Reflections on Life and the Human Experience

---

A lot of people don't get this concept. The world is full of negativity and if you don't stand guard at the door of your mind then people will gladly infect you with their negativity.

Someone once said, "Your association determines your destination." Another wise man opined, "If you fly with pigeons, you will end up becoming one." Another one goes: "If you lie down with dogs, you are going to get up with fleas." Jim Rohn also said succinctly, "You are the average of the five people you hang around the most." Does this ring a bell?

Cold and hot water cannot co-exist in a bucket. One thing will happen for sure: Either the cold water turns the hot water cold or the hot water turns the cold water hot. Almost always, the cold water turns the hot water cold.

The point is, the people you associate with determine how far you get in life. You can't hang around people who slow you down. Sometimes it's okay to leave some people behind. Not everyone will get into the future with you. Be careful, therefore, of your association. They say, "Show me your friend and I will show you your character." Amos 3:3 says, "Can two walk together, except they be agreed?"

Who are your friends? You can't choose your siblings but you can choose your friends. Have an introspection and leave out some people who keep dragging you down. I am attracted to wisdom and so I listen to tapes, read books, talk to and learn from friends who are full of wisdom

Walk with the wise and become wise; if you are already wise, become wiser. It is said that if you are the wisest one in your group, you have to get a new group. Surround yourself with smart people and be challenged to get better every day.

DAY 27

"I owe my success to having listened respectfully to the very best advice, and then going away and doing the exact opposite."

G. K. Chesterton; Writer & Philosopher.

I know I have said earlier, "no one knows enough to be a pessimist". I always ask, how many times have you tried? How long have you been doing it?

How can you possibly know it won't work? An expert they say is someone who knows a lot about very little.

How many times have the experts been wrong? Most of the world's inventions were made when the experts predicted otherwise.

I have a principle, which is, listen but do it anyway. When you listen, you get to learn why they think it's not possible. You can then work your way through it.

When someone offers an advice telling you what you can and cannot do, respectively listen, then go and do it.

They might give you a thousand reasons why it won't work, you only need one reason why it will work. Focus on that on reason.

DAY 28

"If you don't know where you are going, every road will get you nowhere."

Henry Kissinger; Former U.S. Secretary of State.

What do you want? Most people think they know what they really want in life but they don't.

What are you dreaming of? What's your vision? The greatest discovery a man can make in life is to know exactly what he wants and have the courage to move in that direction.

You should therefore be definite about the direction of your life. Don't be distracted by the road others are taking, focus on where you are going. If you don't know where you are going then running faster won't get you there.

Set a SMARTER GOAL for where you are going and then you will get there eventually.

Stay on the path, my mentor says that to me always.

DAY 29

"The gentle strides of the lion should not be mistaken for timidity but a calculated attempt to capture his prey."

African proverb

We often wish things will happen overnight. When we are going after our dreams, it requires a strategy and a daily relentless pursuit. Often, when we don't take time to move, we may crush and lose the dream.

When a lion is in pursuit of its prey, it doesn't just jump on it. When a lion sees an antelope or a deer it's hunting down, it takes some time to plan the attack. Planning is an important part of attaining victory in every endeavor.

In Africa, where wildlife is part of us, this proverb came at the back of farmers and hunters observing a lion hunt down preys. A lion doesn't just spring up on the prey. It may isolate the prey, watch out closely for that one deer it wants to hunt down. Walking carefully and slowly in order not to startle or give away any clues.

When the lion gets to a good position, suddenly it springs into speed and now hunt down its prey.

So, when you are working on your dream, never mistake speed for progress, sometimes movement is movement and speed doesn't matter once you have your focus. Move slow, but focus on the target.

DAY 30

"I am a slow walker ... but I never walk backwards."

Abraham Lincoln; 16TH U.S. President

Direction is much more important than speed. Perhaps events didn't go as fast as you might have wanted during the year. You didn't save as much as you wanted, you didn't do well as you wanted but do you have to stop? No!

It's tough but quitting doesn't make it any easier. Keep moving. One step at a time is better than no step at all.

Movement is movement, no matter how slow or fast. The fact that you are moving means you have every potential to get there, if you don't stop.

Regardless of how the year has gone, don't stop, let us keep walking forward.

DAY 31

"I never waste time looking back."

Eleanor Roosevelt; Politician, Diplomat, Activist & Former First Lady of the U.S.

How did the year go? However, you rate your year, don't spend a second looking back and regretting what you did or didn't do. There is no use for that.

What else can you do? Let me tell you what you can do, you learn your lessons and you look forward to the new year with enthusiasm. You can't change yesterday but remember you can do something today to influence your tomorrow.

So, instead of looking back, face forward. Focus on today. Do what you have to do with what you can and never be satisfied. Be happy but not satisfied because you can be more and you can do more.

There is no time to waste, whatever happened in the year is past. Every success or failure encountered was preparing us for what's ahead so let's focus on conquering what is ahead.

Keep the faith and remember, we shall win, maybe not immediately but definitely.

OTHER BOOKS BY RUDOLPH

BECOMING YOUR DREAM

Have you ever wondered what it takes to make your dreams come true? How do we ensure our dreams do not remain mere wishes?

We never get introduced to the topic as part of our school curricula, from primary school to even higher learning institutions. We are not trained or lectured in our schools on the simple techniques of setting goals, of pursuing our dreams, dealing with adversity and setbacks, of eliminating self-defeating habits and developing positive ones, of using time profitably, of being disciplined and practicing the power of choice, of taking responsibility of our lives, of developing self-confidence, of dealing with loss of dear ones, of turning your dreams to reality, etc. These, we will learn in this book.

This book teaches you to know and define your own dream, believe in yourself, define your short-term goals, then find your path. You must re-evaluate your goals often, and your effort to move forward on your path must be relentless every day. You must also know how to deal with failure: you will have plenty.

The model applies to you whether you are rich or poor, young or old, at any level of education level and at any level of success. Success and winning are not confined to your affluence or your career. Rudolph means the life success of YOU becoming YOUR dream, a dream that includes success for the people around you.

We will win, not immediately, but definitely!!

Available on Amazon. Please visit my Amazon author page.

BECOMING YOUR DREAM
TOMORROW'S STAR
RUDOLPH MENSAH
BECOMING YOUR DREAM
TOMORROW'S STAR
RUDOLPH MENSAH

SET AND ACHIEVE SMARTER GOALS EVERY TIME (GETTING THINGS DONE BOOK 1)

Why is that some people seem to get everything they set out to do done but others never get to finish a single thing?

"Studies reveal that 97% of the people in our society do not have clearly defined goal for their lives", I was part of the 97% until a few years ago when I discovered what it means to have a goal and vision in life. This has changed my life. I am teaching you how to do the same in this small book.

I was a victim, I always had a plan, an idea but it never materialized. I thought about writing a book when I was in Junior High but that was just a wish, in High School, I was part of the school debate team and I wrote poems I really wanted to publish, I was only fantasizing. In college, after being nominated for STUDENT WRITER OF THE YEAR award, I had still not recognized my dream of publishing anything.

Before the year 2016, I developed a new set of skills, I devoted time to study myself and came up with principles to get things done. My word became yes or/and no. if I wanted something done, I knew exactly what to do to get it done. I finally published my first book, 5 months after that I finished writing another soon to be published. Just as the book is about to go out into stores I wrote this one. This one is my third. From a shy kid to now building a strong author brand. Let me show you how I am doing it in this small book.

Well, it's neither magic nor some superhuman qualities needed but there is a public secret which I share in this quick, easy to read and straight to the point book.

Let's learn how to get things done. Life is too short to walk around with unfinished tasks and dreams. We never know how much time we have.

There are so many tomorrows but only one today. Let's learn to get things done every day and live a happy day. Someone once said: "Every day is a good day, if you don't agree, try missing one."

Get the book on my Amazon author page.

SET AND ACHIEVE SMARTER GOALS

A BOOK ON SETTING AND ACHIEVING REALISTIC GOALS EVERY TIME!

Rudolph Mensah | 2017

31 DAYS OF WISDOM

Knowledge is in abundance but wisdom is not. It is very easy to walk around and meet people with academic qualifications, degrees more than that of a thermometer but still devoid of wisdom and common sense.

Many people, especially young folks, are frustrated and are running around with zeal and passion in the wrong directions not knowing exactly what to do and when to do it. Wisdom will show you what to do, when to do and how to do it.

Knowledge is information, wisdom is the application of information, not just application but when and how to apply the information for maximum result.

In this book, 31 DAYS OF WISDOM, I have shared with you practical wisdom in a 31-day devotional guide. Wisdom is not abstract, at least not in this book. I have made it practical for application in our contemporary lives.

This book is meant to be discussed by groups, family devotions, individual meditations, spend time to imbibe the wisdom on every page.

Wisdom is the principal thing therefore get wisdom.

Get the book on my Amazon author page.

RUDOLPH MENSAH
31
DAYS OF
WISDOM
Daily Walk With Wisdom

LEAP: ACTION; THE BRIDGE BETWEEN KNOWING AND DOING (GETTING THINGS DONE Book 2)

It is seemingly easy to get ideas but difficult to make them happen. I get this question the most: When do I start, and when is the best time to start? And my answer is: Leap, Here and Now!

Someone sent me this and I know there are a lot more out there with the same problem: "Hi Rudolph, I like your book on SETTING AND ACHIEVING SMARTER GOALS but my problem is that, regardless of how many goals I set, I never find a way to do what I know I should do. What am I supposed to do? It is not that I don't know what to do, I know exactly what to do, I have all the information but I am always finding it difficult to begin. Beginning always scares me even after months of thinking and planning."

Have you come to a point in life when you know all you should do to succeed but one way or the other success keeps eluding you?

How do we know when it is time to stop analyzing and thinking to move to action? How do we bridge knowing and doing?

A lot of us are stuck at the same place because we have failed to take action on our dreams.

We believe so much in the law of ATTRACTION. We have beautiful imaginations; pretty dreams and we meditate and speak words of affirmations. We believe we will get all we desire just by sitting down and imagining.

One thing the law of ATTRACTION doesn't teach you is in the word ATTRACTION itself. The last six letters of the word spells ACTION.

Action is what will bring you success. The smallest action on your dreams will make a big difference on whether you can achieve your dreams or not.

You may have attended seminars, conferences, got a degree and taken courses but you still seem far away from success. You keep marking time and you never make the step.

I was a self-help junkie and you may be one, too. Always inspired and motivated to do something but never got anything done. You keep listening to all the world's motivational speakers and then what?

Often, we are caught up in a spiral of over-analyzing we never take action. Too much analysis leads to paralysis.

You have read all the books and you keep hiding behind preparation. You can't prepare forever. You have to come out and take action.

There just seems to be this vast gap between what you know and what you actually do and achieve. This is the distance between knowing and doing.

I know many have read a lot of different personal

development and motivational books, blogs and writings. You have learnt a lot about what it takes to succeed. You have developed one action plan after the other. You have a time-line, a plan, a goal but nevertheless, for some reason, after being inspired you can't seem to get past the point where you put the knowledge to action. This breeds a sense of frustration and the conclusion that perhaps such things just don't work, or at least not for you.

Yeah, I know, that is why I wrote this book because I know how it feels to be stuck, that is why I wrote this book. To not only show you how but to get you off your seat to take action on your dreams, NOW!

Get it here: http://a.co/0dtoIzE

Visit my Amazon author page

AMAZON BESTSELLING AUTHOR
OF 31 DAYS OF WISDOM
LEAP
ACTION;
THE
BRIDGE
BETWEEN
KNOWING
AND
DOING
RUDOLPH MENSAH
RUDOLPH MENSAH

PLEASE LEAVE A REVIEW

Did You Like 365 DAYS OF INSPIRATION? Before you go, I would like to say "thank you" for purchasing this book. You could have picked from hundreds of quote books on Amazon but you took a chance to check out this one.

So, a big thank you for buying this book and reading all the way to the end. Now I'd like to ask for a favor.

Could you please take a minute or two and leave a review for this book on Amazon?

This feedback will help me to continue to write the kind of books that help you to stay inspired to take action and get results. And if you loved it, then please rate it five stars and let me know :-)

Will you help me? Leave a review on Amazon.

Please visit my Amazon author page:

www.amazon.com/author/rudolphmensah

Join my mailing list so you don't miss out on my free books and self-development contents:http://eepurl.com/c0KDCf

ABOUT THE AUTHOR

RUDOLPH MENSAH

A young dynamic speaker and lover of God, Rudolph is devoted to helping people find meaning in their lives and become what they dream of. His first book, *BECOMING YOUR DREAM,* has been a first-time sensation globally. He is also the author of the books 31 DAYS OF WISDOM, LEAP: ACTION; THE BRIDGE BETWEEN KNOWING AND DOING and SET AND ACHIEVE SMARTER GOALS EVERY TIME.

He continues to share insight on his website and social media platforms with thousands and speaks to several hundreds of audiences. Rudolph is also a doctor; a job which brings him closer every day to patients' struggles and pain. When medicine can't heal them, he touches them with the special balm of the love of God and a super sense of motivation.

His philosophy in life is that, "life has no meaning until you define it and when you define your life purpose and you put in the work, then you shall win, it may not be immediately but definitely."

He is a native of Elmina in Ghana and continues to work to improve the health of rural communities in Ghana.